DANCE OF ATTACHMENT

Why Smart Women Do Dumb Sh*t in Relationships

and

How to Break the Pattern

Jenn Noble, PCC
Relationship Coach

LUCKY BOOK PUBLISHING

Paperback ISBN: 978-1-997775-13-3
Hardcover ISBN: 978-1-997775-12-6
E-book ISBN: 978-1-997775-11-9

Me: I want my dedication to read...

"To the White Claws, the chocolate, and the weed
that got me to where I am today."

Editor: Doesn't that go against everything you write about in your book? We can't put that, Jenn.

Me: Well then, fine... Just dedicate it to my family... I guess...

MY GIFT TO YOU

You've started the journey, now let's take it further.

The Dance of Attachment Companion Workbook is your guide through Part Two of this book, where you'll learn to D.A.N.C.E. *(trust me, it will make sense when you get there).*

Scan the QR code to download the workbook and get access to all the exercises, prompts, and tools that bring this work to life.

Or go to *danceofattachment.com/workbook* to grab your copy.

This isn't just a book to read. It's a book to move through, one step at a time.

Scan Me

ADVANCE PRAISE

"Of all the books on Attachment, this one is—by far—the most fun to read. Jenn offers a fresh, funny, relatable perspective on women's relationships. The book brings Attachment Theory to life through the compelling metaphor of dance, weaving in stories of heartbreak and healing that are both instructive and empowering."

    – **Dr. Jessie Stern,** Psychologist, Professor, and Author of *Beyond Difficult*

"This is one of the most accessible (and funniest) books on Attachment I've read. A clever balance of science, storytelling, and practical advice, this book will be a go-to for anyone who wants help to understand their relationships and themself."

    – **Rachel Samson,** Clinical Psychologist and Author of *Beyond Difficult*

"This book is pure fucking gold. It's needed in the world because far too many of us are blindly going through life without realizing how our Attachment Styles are shaping and often sabotaging our relationships. For years, I thought I was just crazy, but Jenn shows it's not madness, it's patterns!"

    – **Cheryl Killilea,** No-BS Divorce Coach and CEO of Changing Lanes Wellness

"Jenn has a magical gift of being able to make something as heavy as Attachment feel human, hopeful, and even funny."

    – **Julee Sung,** Career Coach and Author of *Thrive and SHINE*

"As a therapist, I found Dance of Attachment to be an accessible and refreshing take on a topic that can often feel heavy or overly clinical. What struck me most is Jenn's balance of raw honesty with compassion. She doesn't shy away from naming the painful cycles we find ourselves in, yet she continually holds space for hope and change. This book meets people where they are and gently invites them into a new way of relating with themselves and with others."

– **Tannaz Hosseinpour**, Relationship Coach, NLP Practitioner, Registered Psychotherapist (Qualifying), and Author

"Jenn has a gift for making complex psychology feel approachable. Through the metaphor of dance, she explains Attachment Styles in a way that clicks immediately, because we all know what it's like to move in rhythm (or out of step) with someone else. And just as we can recognize the patterns, steps, interactions, and reactions we have become accustomed to, we can also learn new ones that align to what we want more."

– **Vivian Meraki,** Parenting Expert, Somatic Trauma-informed Coach, and Best-selling Author of *Parenting Through Divorce*

"As a therapist trained in trauma and Attachment, I still found so much value in this book. Jenn offers more than another self-help guide. She combines humor with rigor: grounding her insights in research while honoring the healing journey with grace. I found myself nodding, laughing, and feeling seen."

– **Nyle Biondi,** LMFT, Marriage & Family Therapist and Attachment & Chronic Pain Specialist

"This book will absolutely change the way you see yourself and how you show up in relationships. I've broken so many patterns I didn't even realize I had and gained so much confidence in who I am because of Jenn. This book is monumentally life-changing! A must-read for anyone who communicates with and relates to other humans, so basically everyone!"

– **Jordan Harmon,** TEDx Speaker, Artist, and Author of *So Many Animals* and *Paint & Thread*

"Thank you, Jenn, for writing such an honest, refreshing look at how we learn to dance in the first place, that we are NOT locked into that stance and, showing us how to find the dance that is truly ours."

– **Teri Kingston,** TEDx Speaker, Coach and Author of *Get Ready for TED When TED is Ready for You*

"I love how Jenn infuses her own personality and helps us to picture Attachment Styles as dances. Something I can picture and will never forget. Thank you, Jenn, for being courageous enough to share your past and what you have learned so that we can all better our lives through more fulfilling relationships too."

– **Kimberly Brock,** Business Coach & Host of the *She's Just Getting Started* Podcast

"This is not your typical self-help book. Jenn writes this book as if she's talking to a friend—because she is. She's talking to YOU. Get ready to look in the mirror and say 'I see you' in a way you never thought possible."

– **Amanda Richardson,** Co-Founder of *Where in the Park*

AUTHOR'S NOTE

Dear Heartbroken Woman,

I see you.

I know you.

I was you.

I know what it feels like to carry that ache in your chest, wondering why love feels so heavy, so complicated, and so damn hard to get right.

I know what it's like to replay every single fight until the words feel like daggers, to stare at your phone waiting for a text that never comes, and to lie awake at night asking yourself that brutal question: *What's wrong with me?*

And yeah... I know what it's like to do dumb sh*t in the name of love. To drive past his house just to see if the lights are on. To stay in that relationship you know isn't good for you because you're terrified of being alone.

To send that "one last text" that you swore you wouldn't send. To bend yourself into a pretzel trying to be "easy," "chill," or "low-maintenance," only to end up feeling more unseen than ever. Stuff you promised yourself you'd never do again, but somehow... there you were.

But here's the truth I NEED you to hear: There is nothing wrong with you. Read that again. **Nothing**. The pain you've carried, the patterns you've repeated, and the heartbreak that has weighed you down all make sense once you understand where they come from. What most women don't realize in the middle of the mess is that it does not have to stay this way. The way you love today is not the way you are destined to love forever. Patterns can be rewritten. Stories can be retold. You are allowed to choose differently, and you are more than capable of doing it.

I wrote this book for you. For the woman who knows she's smart, capable, and strong but can't figure out why relationships leave her feeling small, insecure, and unsure of herself. For the woman who wants more (more connection, more safety, more love that lasts) but has no idea where to begin.

Healing is possible. It's messy, it's brave, and it's absolutely worth every single step. This book isn't about fixing you, because you are not broken. It's about helping you see the dances you've been caught in, the steps you learned without even realizing it, and giving you the tools to choreograph something new.

You don't have to keep dancing to someone else's tune. You don't have to keep repeating patterns that never served you in the first place. You get to take the lead, you get to choose your rhythm, and you get to create a love that actually feels safe and fulfilling.

And I'm here to show you how.

Yours in Support,
Jenn

TABLE OF CONTENTS

PART ONE
Learn Your Choreography 1

PART TWO
Rewire Your Rhythm 73

LAST DANCE
Last Chance for Love 179

HOW TO USE THIS BOOK

Alright, so here's the deal.

Attachment Styles? They're not exactly the easiest thing to wrap your head around. I mean, "Attachment Theory" sounds more like something you'd hear in a grad-level psych class. Not the key to figuring out why you're spiraling over a text he didn't send.

But as an ICF-accredited Relationship Coach, TEDx speaker, and host of the *Speak Honest* podcast, I've helped thousands of women finally understand why love feels so damn hard AND more importantly, what to do about it.

And before I ever taught this stuff? I lived it. Messy, spirally, mascara-streaked and all. That's why I plan to explain Attachment Theory the same way I do to my clients: as dances.

Yep. **Dances**.

Because relationships are kind of like choreography. You've got your rhythm, your moves, your patterns... and sometimes? Your toes get stepped on. A lot. So let's get clear on the language before we dive in.

You've probably heard of "Attachment Styles." Anxious, Avoidant, Disorganized, and Secure. Those are the terms you'll see all over Tik-Tok, Instagram, or in your group chats after a breakup.

But in this book, I'm going to call them something slightly different: **Adapted Attachment Stances.**

Why? Because you weren't born with a "style." It's not last season's straight leg jeans *(FYI: Thank GOD flare jeans came back in style, am I right?!)* You **adapted** to the love you had access to. You developed a stance, a posture, a pattern, a way of relating that helped you stay safe, get connection, or protect your heart. Let's be honest, sometimes those stances saved you. But now they might be keeping you stuck.

Mary Main, one of the key researchers behind Attachment Theory, described these patterns as "**stances**." Ways we learn to show up in relationships based on our earliest bonds. And Dr. Dan Siegel refers to these as "**adaptations**," because they aren't fixed traits. They're responses. They're learned.

That means you can unlearn them too. The beauty of a dance is that you can always learn new moves, ones that don't leave you stepping on toes but actually let you enjoy the music.

So, while I'll still use the phrase "Attachment Styles" from time to time *(just so we're speaking the same language)*, I want you to start thinking of your patterns as stances. Adapted ways of moving through your relationships that kept you safe once, but might be hurting you now.

Oh, and bonus thought... Stance rhymes with **Dance**. Which, let's be honest, makes all my metaphors work even better.

Coincidence? I think not.

PART ONE: LEARN YOUR CHOREOGRAPHY

In Part One, we'll explore the four main Adapted Attachment Stances. These are the dances you learned long before you could walk:

- **Salsa of Uncertainty** (Anxious), where you chase love like it's oxygen and fear every move your partner makes.

- **Solo Tango** (Avoidant), where independence is everything and closeness feels like a threat.

- **Pendulum Swing Dance** (Disorganized), where you long for intimacy one moment and push it away the next.

- **Smooth Waltz** (Secure), where trust, safety, and balance take the lead.

These dances shape how you love, fight, pull away, cling, and what your nervous system does every time things get too close or not close enough. They're not random. They're patterned. And once you see them, you can start to change them.

I'll show you where this choreography comes from, why your nervous system learned them in the first place, and how it's been trying to keep you safe *(even if it doesn't feel that way now).*

You'll begin to recognize your own moves in these patterns, connect the dots between your past and your present, and finally understand why love has felt the way it has and why it doesn't always have to stay that way.

PART TWO: REWIRE YOUR RHYTHM

In Part Two, you'll learn how to D.A.N.C.E. *(Not the ballroom kind, though if you want to waltz in your kitchen, I support that.)* The process I teach for rewiring the rhythm that guides how you show up in love.

D ISCOVER YOUR ATTACHMENT STANCE

When you read Part One of this book, you're already 20% of the way there. *(Look at you go!)*

A LLEVIATE YOUR ATTACHMENT WOUNDS

The ones that whisper, "I am not enough," "I am too much," or "I am worthless." We're flipping that script, girl.

N URTURE YOUR ATTACHMENT NEEDS

You. Are. Not. Needy. I can't wait to teach you how to stop apologizing for your needs and start honoring them.

C OMMUNICATE WITH CONFIDENCE

Because once you get the hang of it? Girl, you're going to say what you mean, mean what you say, and do it all without spiraling.

E MBODY SECURE ATTACHMENT

This is where it gets real. This is where you stop performing and start aligning with the version of you who feels safe, seen, and secure in your relationships.

Step by step you will learn a new rhythm that feels natural, safe, and true. Each part of the D.A.N.C.E. brings you closer to the version of yourself who no longer questions her worth, silences her needs, or fears closeness. Make this the rhythm you come home to.

ABOUT THOSE LITTLE NUMBERS

You'll notice little superscript numbers throughout this book. No, they're not typos or some weird formatting glitch. Those numbers are citations. They connect to the endnotes section at the back of the book, where I've listed every study, journal article, and research source that backs up what I'm saying.

Because here's the thing: nothing makes my eye twitch harder than when someone vaguely claims "research says" without telling you WHAT research. As someone who's both lived through Attachment struggles and studies them professionally, I took great care to ground everything in this book in solid science.

The endnotes section is my gift to fellow research geeks who want to dive deeper into the studies behind the stories and strategies. You don't need to check every reference to benefit from this book, but they're there if you want them because your healing journey deserves more than just "trust me, bro" advice.

And if you're not a research lover, don't worry. You can skip the numbers and keep reading without missing a beat. Think of the end-notes as a bonus track. You know, like the secret song that used to pop up at the end of a CD. *(If you have no idea what I'm talking about, just smile and keep reading. The rest of us are over here feeling ancient.)*

Consider it extra insight for the curious, the skeptics, or anyone who *(like me)* loves knowing there is data behind the dance.

DISCLAIMER

While I have tried to speak from the heart of my own lived experience, I know it reflects only one slice of the human story. Throughout this book, you will see me predominantly address cisgender, heterosexual women in relationships with men. That is the world I know most intimately.

I want to fully honor that love, Attachment, and human connection take many forms and that each is worthy of equal dignity. If you find yourself outside the specific focus of these pages, my hope is that you will still find resonance in the inner patterns and Attachment dynamics described here. These truths extend far beyond gender and orientation.

Attachment at its core is about being human. Whether you are single, partnered, queer, trans, non-binary, polyamorous, or somewhere in between, the heartbeat of Attachment is universal. We all know the ache of disconnection. We all know the pull toward closeness. And we all share the deep, undeniable need to feel safe, seen, and secure in our relationships.

For readers who want a more expansive approach to Attachment, I highly recommend works such as *Polysecure* by Jessica Fern, *The Power of Attachment* by Diane Poole Heller, and *Attachment Theory in Action* by Sue Johnson.

My deepest hope is to write more books in the future that speak to the wider spectrum of human relationships. For now, this book is written for women who are in (or who long for) relationships with men. I offer it with respect, compassion, and a commitment to honoring the diversity of all lived experiences.

HOW TO MAKE THE MOST OF THIS BOOK

This book is designed to walk with you, not rush you. Each part builds on the last, and the journey is meant to be taken at your own pace. To help you along the way, here is how to make the most of this book.

1. Start with **Part One** to figure out your current dance moves.

2. Then head to **Part Two** when you're ready to learn new ones.

3. Take your time. Healing is a **journey**, not a destination.

4. Revisit the pieces that **speak** to you and skip around when you need to.

5. Use the reflection prompts, write in the margins, cry if you need to. You're **safe** here.

6. Get extra support *(because you don't have to do this alone)* at *danceofattachment.com/resources*. This is where you can find worksheets, guided meditations, and **community** support waiting for you.

7. Want to dive even deeper? Watch my full **TEDx Talk**: *Do Attachment Styles Determine the Dance of Our Relationships?* Visit *danceofattachment.com/tedx* to check it out.

You don't need to be perfect. You just need to be willing. This is your journey, and I'm so honored to be a small part of it.

PART ONE

LEARN YOUR CHOREOGRAPHY

"Great dancers are not great because of their technique, they are great because of their passion."
- Martha Graham

INTRODUCTION

I didn't just get dumped.

I got **emotionally ejected** from my entire sense of reality while black-out high on a Tuesday, eating a melted chocolate bar and chasing it with a warm White Claw like it was communion.

People say 2020 was hard and sad for everyone. I get it. But girl... I wasn't just sad, I was SAAAAD sad. Capital S. Ugly crying. Snot-bubble. Full-blown identity crisis while doomscrolling YouTube and desperately searching "how to get him back" like love was a lost AirPod.

I wasn't okay. And I didn't even have the language for why.

Everyone else was baking sourdough and reorganizing their closets, and I was sitting in my own stanky funk asking the universe if I was just... fundamentally **unlovable**. And then, somewhere between YouTube tarot readings and a playlist called "songs to cry in the shower to," I stumbled across a video on Attachment Styles.

And suddenly... it all made sense.

The chasing, the panicking. The why-do-I-feel-crazy energy that hit every time he pulled away. The way I shapeshifted into the "cool girl" just to hold on to someone who never actually saw me. The way I confused intensity with intimacy. The way I begged to be chosen without ever asking if I even wanted him.

Here's the thing: every one of those choices looked "desperate" from the outside, but inside they made perfect sense. My body thought closeness was **survival**. My brain thought that being chosen meant I was safe. So of course I chased, clung, bargained, twisted myself into knots. I wasn't broken. I was doing what I had been trained to do. This is what it means to have an Attachment Wound. Your nervous system goes into overdrive to keep love close, even if it costs you your dignity, your peace, and your sense of self.

Like the time I baked my ex a homemade cake for his birthday less than a month after he dumped me. I told myself it was kind, mature, proof that I was the "cool ex." But really, I thought a Funfetti cake could somehow erase the breakup and win him back. That is Anxious Attachment at its finest, confusing over-giving with love and hoping that being selfless enough would finally make me feel worthy enough.

It was never just about him though. It was about every version of me that was still aching to feel like I was **enough**. That's when it clicked. I wasn't broken. I was caught in a dance I had been taught but never agreed to.

And this? This book right here? It's not just about relationships. It's about that **dance**. The one your nervous system choreographed without asking you first. The one that kept you small, Anxious, Avoidant, confused, over-giving, under-receiving, and so fucking tired.

Yes, I'll share a few studies here and there. Especially the ones that made me stop and go, wait... this is me. But don't worry. This isn't some dry psychology textbook. I'm explaining everything through dance metaphors. Like the Smooth Waltz, the Salsa of Uncertainty, the Solo Tango, and the Pendulum Swing Dance.

Because love isn't a diagnosis. **It's a rhythm.**

And if you've been stepping on toes, or getting yours stomped on, I got you. We're going to unpack all of it. The kind of love you learned. The beliefs you picked up about who you had to be in order to be chosen. And most importantly, how to rewrite that story into something honest, healthy, and finally yours.

This is the book I needed that night in bed. This is the map I didn't have when I thought the only way to be loved was to earn it. And now I'm handing it to you.

Let's figure out your dance. Let's change the song. Let's find your rhythm. Because, babes, you were NEVER the problem. You were just dancing to someone else's beat.

So... take a deep breath. Wipe the mascara off your cheeks. Kick off the shoes that were never made for you in the first place. And when you're ready, I'll be right here. Hand outstretched, smirk on my face, heart wide open.

We'll take it slow at first. I'll lead. You just breathe. This time, you don't have to twist yourself into knots to be held. This time, the dance isn't yours to learn alone. This time, you get to move like you were always meant to.

So, what do you say?

Will you take my hand... and dance with me?

BEFORE WE DANCE

Before we dive into the Salsa of Uncertainty, Solo Tango, Pendulum Swing Dance, or Smooth Waltz, let's pause for a second and ask...

What the hell is Attachment Theory, anyway?

At its core, Attachment Theory is the science of how we connect. It explains the emotional blueprint you developed in childhood and how it dictates your love, safety, and relationships.

British psychologist John Bowlby was one of the first to explore this. He believed that humans are biologically wired to seek connection with a caregiver because connection equals survival.[1] When that connection is consistent and safe, the child learns that people can be trusted and that love is reliable.

Bowlby's colleague, psychologist Mary Ainsworth, built on this theory and ran an experiment called the *Strange Situation* in the 1970s.[2] She watched how babies reacted when their caregiver left the room and then came back. From this, she identified **three** distinct patterns:

1. **Secure**: Baby is upset when mom leaves but is easily soothed when she returns.

2. **Anxious (or Ambivalent)**: Baby clings and cries, but can't calm down even when mom comes back.

3. **Avoidant**: Baby doesn't seem bothered when mom leaves and avoids her when she returns.

So those are the OG categories we now refer to as "Attachment Styles."

But here's where it gets more interesting and more accurate. In the late 1980s, researchers Mary Main and Judith Solomon were reviewing recordings from the *Strange Situation* experiment when they noticed something didn't quite fit. Some babies would approach their caregiver and then freeze. Others would reach out, then suddenly pull away. Their behavior was disorganized, contradictory, and clearly rooted in fear.[3]

So they introduced a fourth pattern.

Drumroll please... **Disorganized Attachment.**

This one is often linked to trauma, neglect, or caregivers who were frightening or unpredictable. And that's why it's so damn confusing in adult relationships. It's a push-pull dance of "I want closeness, ew no I don't... this is scary, now go away... but wait, why did you go away? I really wanted that closeness, come back! Ew no... don't come back... gross... why did you come back, you weirdo?"

Yeah. It's a lot. But that, my friend, is Disorganized Attachment in a nutshell.

In this book, we're going to look at all four patterns but not just as "styles." Remember, we're calling them **Adapted Attachment Stances** because these aren't fixed labels or personality types. They're protective postures that your nervous system learned to survive love that didn't always feel safe.

This language honors the work of Mary Main, who described these patterns as stances, and Dr. Dan Siegel, who refers to them as adaptations. Their research laid the foundation for everything you're about to learn. I'm just here to break it down in a way that feels human, hopeful, and *(let's be real)* way more fun to read.

And just to be clear, these are **NOT** personality types; we aren't trying to decode your sun sign with a wing of Meyers–Briggs *(Though if you're wondering, I'm a Gemini, 4w3, INFP—Obviously.)* These are adaptive coping strategies that your nervous system developed to SURVIVE the emotional climate of your early years.

And thanks to modern neuroscience, we now know that your brain isn't stuck with these old patterns forever.[4] Through intentional healing, consistency, and self-compassion, your brain can literally rewire itself.[5] *(Which is pretty fucking cool if you ask me.)*

So if your relationships keep falling apart, if you're always the one overthinking, or if you feel like love equals anxiety or walking on eggshells... you are not a lost cause.

You're just dancing the steps taught to you. And now? You can learn new ones. You've been stuck doing the "Macarena" when all you wanted to do was the "Cha Cha Slide." Let's teach you the "Cha Cha Slide" girl, because it is so much nicer than those weird hand movements...

*(Also, be honest... Did you just start doing the "Macarena" in your head? They **are** weird, right?!)*

One

SALSA OF UNCERTAINTY
ANXIOUS ATTACHMENT

The Anxious person doesn't just want to be loved, they need proof every five minutes that they still are.

The text came in at 7:03 p.m.

"Hey, can we raincheck tonight? Work stuff came up."

Emily stared at her phone already halfway through curling her hair, already two glasses of wine deep for "courage," already having rehearsed the casual-but-cute stories she planned to tell him about her week. The pit in her stomach opened like a sinkhole.

This wasn't just disappointment. This was devastation.

7:04 PM: *Is he lying? Did I say something wrong?*

7:06 PM: *He's probably with that girl from his Instagram. The one with the hiking photos. I knew it.*

7:09 PM: *Should I respond? What's the right amount of cool vs. caring? What's the perfect text that will make him still like me?*

7:12 PM: *Maybe if I had been more fun last time. Maybe if I hadn't mentioned my family stuff.*

7:15 PM: *I should probably just break up with him before he breaks up with me.*

7:18 PM: *Actually, I'll say it's totally fine and then be extra sweet and plan something special for next time.*

By 7:30 she had spiraled through an entire relationship apocalypse, drafted *(and deleted)* seventeen different responses, texted three friends for advice, and googled "how to know if he's losing interest." All while her curling iron burned a perfect half-moon shape into her bathroom counter.

What she couldn't see then was that this wasn't about this guy, or his text, or even this night.

This was the **Salsa of Uncertainty** in full swing.

WELCOME TO ANXIOUS ATTACHMENT

Let's talk about **Anxious Attachment**. If you've ever felt like your entire emotional world hinges on someone else's affection, if your heart races when they take too long to respond, if you constantly worry about being "too much" or "not enough," then welcome to the club nobody actually wants to join.

Anxious Attachment is one of the three main Nonsecure Adapted Attachment Stances, characterized by a deep fear of abandonment, an intense craving for closeness, and a tendency to prioritize relationships above almost everything else in your life. People with Anxious Attachment often have an uncanny "spidey sense" for emotional distance. You can detect the slightest shift in someone's tone, the subtlest change in their texting pattern, the most microscopic hint that they might be pulling away. It's your emotional superpower and your kryptonite all at once.

This hyperawareness is exhausting. It's like you're always on high alert, waiting for the other shoe to drop, waiting for the person you care about to realize you're not worth sticking around for. Sound familiar?

That's why I call Anxious Attachment the **Salsa of Uncertainty**.

Picture a salsa dance floor. While everyone else seems to be moving effortlessly with their partners, the Anxiously Attached dancer is performing a completely different routine. They're vibrant and intense, yes, but they're also frantically trying to stay in perfect rhythm with their partner, constantly checking for approval, desperately trying to anticipate the next move before it happens.

This dancer isn't enjoying the music or the movement. They're scanning for danger, analyzing every step, overthinking every turn. *Did I step wrong? Are they getting bored with me? Are they looking at other dancers? Should I try harder? Should I let go?* The internal dialogue never stops.

That's the exhausting rhythm of Anxious Attachment. Have you ever found yourself obsessively checking your phone, mentally rehearsing conversations that haven't happened yet, or burning a perfect half-moon shape into your bathroom counter with a curling iron while drafting seventeen different responses to a simple cancellation text?

If so, you might just be dancing the **Salsa of Uncertainty**. And you are far from alone. This dance is more common than you think, even if nobody talks about it.

THE SCIENCE OF OVERTHINKING

Here's what's actually happening in your brain and body when you're in Anxious Attachment mode.

Remember Mary Ainsworth's *Strange Situation* experiment from the 1970s? When she studied how babies responded to their mothers leaving and returning to a room, she found that Anxiously Attached babies were incredibly distressed when their mothers left, but here's the kicker: they remained distressed even when mom came back. They wanted comfort but couldn't be soothed by it.[1]

As Ainsworth noted, they "often worry that their partner doesn't really love them or won't want to stay with them."[2] Sound familiar?

Fast forward to adulthood, and research by psychologists Cindy Hazan and Phillip Shaver found that roughly 19% of adults fall into the Anxious Attachment category or at least have these tendencies.[3] That's nearly **one in five** people walking around with nervous systems primed for abandonment, constantly scanning for threats to connection.

What's happening in your brain? The **amygdala** *(your emotional alarm system)* goes into overdrive. According to neuropsychologist Dr. Louis Cozolino, people with Anxious Attachment show increased activity in the brain's threat-detection circuits.[4]

That means your Attachment Stance isn't just activated... it's on constant red alert, scanning for even the slightest sign that connection might be fading. Every pause, every sigh, every unanswered text? Feels like danger.

THE PHYSICAL COST OF UNCERTAINTY

The Anxious Attachment dance doesn't just happen in your mind. It shows up in your body too.

When you're stuck in the **Salsa of Uncertainty**, your body pumps out cortisol and adrenaline like it's hosting a stress hormone kegger.

Your heart races, your breathing gets shallow, your digestion goes haywire. According to Dr. Gabor Maté's research on the body-mind connection, this kind of chronic stress can lead to real, long-term health issues.[5]

And it's not just theory. A 2010 study at the University of Toronto found that people with Anxious Attachment showed higher levels of **inflammation** and reported more physical symptoms when under relationship stress.[6] Your body literally hurts from loving so hard.

CHOREOGRAPHY OF THE SALSA OF UNCERTAINTY

So how do you know if you're dancing the Salsa of Uncertainty? Time to break down the signature moves:

The Hypervigilance Hip Sway
This is where you become a relationship detective, analyzing every text, facial expression, and tone shift. *He usually puts an exclamation point here. Something must be wrong.*

The Reassurance Rumba
The constant need for validation and confirmation that everything is okay. *Do you love me? Are you mad? Are we good?* The Anxious person doesn't just want to be loved, they need proof every five minutes that they still are.

The Protest Pirouette
When you don't get the connection you crave, you might act out to get attention through conflict, drama, or by threatening the relationship. *Maybe if I break up with him, he'll finally show he cares.*

The People-Pleasing Paso Doble

Becoming whoever you think your partner wants you to be, often at the expense of your own needs, boundaries, and identity. *I told him I love horror movies, but actually, they give me nightmares. I just didn't want to seem boring.*

These moves aren't random. According to Attachment researcher Phillip Shaver, these protest behaviors—like over-texting, people-pleasing, or picking fights—are remarkably consistent across cultures and age groups.[7] They're not just "bad habits." They're your nervous system's attempt to restore connection when it senses a threat. It's survival choreography, not personal failure.

ORIGINS OF ANXIOUS: BEYOND CLINGY

You didn't just wake up one day and decide to text your date seven times in a row. This dance was choreographed long before you downloaded dating apps.

According to John Bowlby's Attachment Theory, your first relationships, usually with your parents or primary caregivers, create **templates** for how you expect all future relationships to work.[8] If your early care was inconsistent, unpredictable, or conditional, your brain learned a crucial lesson: love is unreliable, and you have to work hard to keep it.

Maybe you had a parent who was emotionally available sometimes but checked out other times. Maybe big emotions were met with withdrawal instead of comfort. Maybe you learned that being "too much" meant people would leave, so you tried to be **perfect** instead.

As Dr. Brené Brown says, "We are biologically, cognitively, physically, and spiritually wired for connection."[9] When that connection feels threatened in childhood, your system adapts to try to secure it, even if those adaptations don't serve you as an adult.

AMBER'S DANCE: THE GOOD GIRL

"I don't understand it, Jenn."

Amber, a client who came to me after her third devastating breakup in two years, was in tears.

"I give everything to my relationships. I'm always available, always supportive, always trying to make them happy. Why do they always leave?"

As we explored her relationships in her childhood, a pattern emerged. Amber's mom had struggled with depression, which meant some days she was emotionally present and loving, and other days she couldn't get out of bed. Young Amber never knew which version of her mother she'd get when she came home from school.

"I learned to read her moods instantly," Amber explained. "I'd walk in and within seconds, I could tell if it was a good day or a bad day. If it was good, I'd try to keep it that way by being extra helpful, extra sweet, extra everything. If it was bad, I'd try to fix it. I'd make her tea, tell her funny stories from school, anything to pull her out of it."

And Amber was **REALLY** good at pulling her mom out of her dark moods. The problem is she was a little TOO good at it, and it taught her a few things.

This childhood experience taught Amber **three** crucial lessons:

1. Love is inconsistent and unpredictable.
2. It's her responsibility to manage other people's emotions.
3. If someone withdraws, she must work harder to win them back.

No wonder Amber's adult relationships followed the same painful pattern. She was hyper-attuned to any slight change in her partner's mood or behavior. She'd exhaust herself trying to be "perfect" to keep them happy. And when they naturally needed space, she'd panic and double down on her efforts to maintain connection. Often pushing them further away.

It wasn't that Amber didn't know how to love. She loved deeply, fiercely, with her whole heart. The issue was that her love always came with an undercurrent of fear. Fear that if she stopped giving, stopped fixing, stopped proving herself, the love would vanish just like it had in her childhood.

That fear didn't just live in her mind; it lived in her nervous system. Every unread text, every sigh from a partner, every night they seemed distracted triggered the same alarm bells she'd felt as a child walking through the door, bracing herself for which version of her mother she'd meet that day.

Amber was dancing the **Salsa of Uncertainty** with every partner, just as she had with her mother. And like so many with Anxious Attachment, she was drawn to partners who reinforced this familiar, painful dynamic, keeping the cycle alive no matter how hard she tried to break free.

Coach's Note: The Anxious-Avoidant Dance

Here's a fun fact that's not actually fun at all: people with Anxious Attachment are often magnetically drawn to partners with Avoidant Attachment. It's what therapist Dr. Sue Johnson calls the pursue-withdraw dance.[10] It's the kind of dance that feels electric at first, but underneath it's pure anxiety in disguise.

You, as the Anxious partner, sense emotional distance and move closer, seeking reassurance. Your Avoidant partner feels suffocated and backs away. This confirms your worst fear *(they're leaving!)*, so you pursue even more intensely, which makes them withdraw further...

And round and round we go on the relationship merry-go-round from hell. It feels dramatic, but to your body it feels normal. The push and pull becomes addictive, even when it hurts.

What feels chaotic to the outside world feels like oxygen to your nervous system.

This isn't just something I've noticed in my coaching practice *(and trust me, I see it all the time)*, it's backed by research. Psychologist Phillip Shaver observed that "people with Avoidant Attachment Styles are likely to be paired with Anxious lovers, a pairing that often leads to considerable unhappiness in both partners."[11] It feels like chemistry, but it's really survival patterns reenacting themselves. When love feels like a cycle of fear and distance, we don't recognize it as a problem. We recognize it as home.

FROM UNCERTAIN TO STEADY

Here's the good news. And it's really, really good news. Your Adapted Attachment Stance is **not a life sentence** of emotional chaos. Thanks to neuroplasticity (the brain's ability to rewire itself), you can absolutely learn new dance steps.

As neuropsychologist Donald Hebb proposed back in 1949, when one neuron repeatedly activates another, the connection between them strengthens over time. This principle is often summed up by the popular phrase, "Neurons that fire together, wire together."[12]

In **Part Two** of this book, we'll learn how to work with your brain, not against it. You'll discover how to create new neural patterns through consistent, safe, and emotionally corrective experiences. The goal isn't just to think differently; it's to wire differently. Because when you change how your nervous system responds to love, connection, and conflict, the dance changes too.

SPEAK HONEST: DANCING WITH MY DISAPPOINTMENT

I had been counting down to this night like a kid waiting for Christmas morning. The lights, the music, the chance to blend my worlds and have my boyfriend join my son and me made it feel so special. I pictured us laughing together, sipping hot cocoa, taking in the festive magic as a little family. Just the three of us, making memories I thought we'd hold onto forever.

Then, just as I was getting everyone ready, the text came. My stomach dropped before I even opened it.

"Hey, I know I said I would go to the thing, but I had a really rough day and I need to go to bed."

I stared at my phone, feeling like the air had been sucked out of the room. *What?* He couldn't be serious. We'd talked about this for weeks; this was supposed to be special. I had been counting down the days. And now? Everything felt like it was falling apart.

The anxiety kicked in hard. I started questioning everything. *Did I say something wrong? Did I expect too much? Why did I get so excited in the first place?* The usual spiral set in.

I called a friend, but the more I talked about it, the worse I felt. I couldn't shake the feeling of rejection. Instead of calming down, I started blowing the situation up in my head, making it way bigger than it really was. "No worries!" I texted back, pretending like everything was fine, but it obviously wasn't.

I carried it like a bruise. Held onto it for weeks and let it poison the space between us. But it didn't just stay between me and him. It bled into the night with my son. What should have been a fun evening together turned into me spiraling, distracted, and stuck in my disappointment.

I couldn't be present with my son because I was too caught up in the empty space beside me, the story in my head that I had been **rejected**. One moment that could have passed quietly instead ruined weeks of my relationship and stole a night of joy from my kid—all because of my Anxious Attachment.

The **Salsa of Uncertainty** isn't just exhausting for you; it throws off the rhythm for everyone around you. It's like trying to dance with someone who's out of sync. Your nervous system leads the dance, but it pulls everyone else out of step, leaving the whole dance floor feeling chaotic and offbeat.

YOUR TURN: SALSA OF UNCERTAINTY REFLECTION QUESTIONS

1. Think about your last relationship "spiral." What triggered it? What stories did you tell yourself? What did you feel in your body?

2. What's your go-to "protest behavior" when you feel disconnected from someone you care about?

3. Can you identify patterns from your early life that might have shaped your Anxious Attachment?

4. What's one small way you could respond differently next time your Anxious Attachment gets triggered?

Remember, the goal isn't to never feel Anxiously Attached again. The goal is to **feel** the sadness, the anger, and the disappointment; and then make choices based on your values rather than your fears. And eventually, with practice and patience, to find a rhythm that feels less like desperate grasping and more like confident connection. You may have learned the **Salsa of Uncertainty**, but sweetheart, that doesn't have to be your forever dance.

Two

SOLO TANGO
AVOIDANT ATTACHMENT

The problem isn't your self-sufficiency, it's that this strength has become your only strategy.

The email landed in Jamie's inbox with a soft ping.

"Hey beautiful, just checking in since I haven't heard from you in a few days. Still on for dinner Friday? Miss your face. x"

Jamie stared at her screen, a wave of discomfort washing over her. Three weeks ago, this message would have made her smile. Now it felt like hands around her throat.

Her finger hovered over the reply button. What was wrong with her? Dave was smart, successful, kind, and clearly into her. They'd been dating for almost two months, the longest she'd made it in years. Her friends thought he was perfect.

But something had shifted after their last date. They'd shared a bottle of wine, and in the warm glow of her living room, Dave had looked at her with soft eyes and said, "I think I'm falling for you, Jamie."

Seven simple words. But in the days since, she had felt like she was drowning.

She hadn't replied to his last three texts. She had canceled plans last weekend, claiming she was too busy due to work deadlines. And now, staring at this perfectly reasonable email, all she could think was, *I need to end this before it gets worse.*

The same suffocating feeling was creeping in. The same urge to run. The same rehearsed script forming in her mind, *You're amazing, but I'm just not in the right place for something serious right now.*

It wasn't even a lie. She never seemed to be in the right place. But deep down, Jamie wondered if a place like that even existed for her.

What she couldn't see then was that this wasn't about Dave, or his feelings, or even that particular moment.

This was the **Solo Tango** in full force.

WELCOME TO AVOIDANT ATTACHMENT

Let's talk about **Avoidant Attachment**. If you've ever felt that stomach-dropping panic when someone gets too close, if you prize your independence above nearly everything, if intimacy feels both desirable and dangerous...

Welcome to another club nobody consciously signs up for.

Avoidant Attachment is the next up on our list of the three main Nonsecure Adapted Attachment Stances, characterized by a deep discomfort with emotional intimacy, a fierce need for self-sufficiency, and a tendency to create distance when relationships deepen. People with Avoidant Attachment often appear confident and self-contained on the outside. You might be the friend who's always there for others but rarely asks for help yourself. The partner who needs "space" when things get serious. The person others describe as "mysterious" or "hard to read."

But beneath that composed exterior? There's often a complex world of emotions kept carefully contained. It's not that you don't feel. It's that feelings, especially vulnerable ones, feel threatening.

That's why I call Avoidant Attachment the **Solo Tango**.

Picture a tango. It typically requires two people, moving in passionate, precise coordination. But the Avoidantly Attached dancer is performing their own version. They're elegant and controlled, yes, but they're dancing **alone**. Even when they have a partner, they maintain a careful distance, leading the dance with precise steps that keep emotional intimacy at bay.

This dancer isn't cold or unfeeling. They're self-protective. *What if I let them lead and they step on my toes? What if I follow their moves and look foolish? What if I give up control and can't get it back?* The fears run deep.

Have you ever found yourself pulling away just when a relationship starts to get deeper? Maybe you've created unnecessary conflict, or suddenly started focusing on your partner's small flaws when things felt too close? If you've caught yourself in these patterns, you're not alone. Around **25% of adults** experience behaviors linked to Avoidant Attachment[1], often resulting in the **Solo Tango**. A pattern where they unconsciously maintain emotional distance, even when they desire connection.

THE SCIENCE OF SELF-PROTECTION

So, what's really going on underneath that calm, composed exterior when you're in Avoidant Attachment mode? It's more than just emotional distance. It's a complex system of defenses and **self-protective mechanisms** working overtime to keep vulnerability at bay.

Think of Avoidant Attachment as the emotional equivalent of an iceberg. Above the surface, everything looks fine—cool, calm, collected, and fiercely independent. But below that surface is a deep, hidden world of alerts and defense mechanisms designed to block emotional closeness.

When it comes to Avoidant Attachment, it's like a perfectly composed exterior masking inner tension. Infants classified as Avoidant often appear unfazed when separated from their caregivers. They don't cry, don't seek comfort, and seem totally fine. Almost like they've got it all together. But what's really happening is that they've learned to suppress their emotions to protect themselves from the **vulnerability** of emotional connection.

In contrast, Secure infants show a more open response to stress. When their caregiver leaves, they cry and express their discomfort. But the key difference is that during the reunion, they're quickly soothed by their caregiver, knowing that their emotional needs will be met.[2] This ability to express distress and receive comfort reinforces their **sense of security**, strengthening their trust that their caregiver will be there when they need them most. Avoidant infants, on the other hand, hold back from expressing their emotions because they've learned that doing so doesn't always lead to the reassurance they need.

Fast forward to adulthood and this same disconnection between the external appearance and internal experience persists. Your partner might say something that hurts you deeply, yet your face will show nothing. Your colleague might praise your work and you brush it off casually. Your new relationship starts getting serious but that's when you suddenly develop an intense interest in anything else.

This isn't coldness. It's protection in action.

Brain imaging studies show that Avoidant individuals tend to suppress emotional responses by reducing activity in brain regions associated with emotional processing, such as the anterior insula and cingulate cortex[3] *(fancy words for parts of the brain that help us with emotions and decision making)*. These areas are involved in emotional regulation and **Attachment-related distress**. Your brain essentially "turns down the volume" on feelings that might lead to vulnerability or dependence. It's a sophisticated defense mechanism, but it comes at a cost—creating emotional distance and difficulty with intimacy.

THE PHYSICAL PRICE OF INDEPENDENCE

Your mind can trick itself into believing you're fine alone, but your body keeps tabs.

That tightness in your chest when someone says, "I miss you"? The sudden exhaustion after an intimate conversation? The mysterious physical symptoms that appear during relationship stress? That's your body speaking the emotional truth your words won't allow.

Dr. Stephen Porges calls this state "autonomic incongruence." When your external expression and internal experience are fundamentally mismatched.[4] Your nervous system gets stuck in a paradox: simultaneously activating connection-seeking circuits and danger-responding circuits. It's like pressing the gas and the brakes at the same time, and eventually your whole system feels worn down. No wonder it's exhausting.

Studies show that Avoidant individuals often experience:

- **Elevated stress hormones** even when they look calm, indicating that emotional suppression takes a biological toll.[5]

- Increased physical **health issues** during relationship conflicts, with stress manifesting in various somatic symptoms like headaches or digestive problems.[6]

- Higher levels of **unexplained physical symptoms**, which are often linked to unresolved emotional stress.[7]

- Greater cognitive load required to process emotional information, making it **harder to manage** complex emotional situations.[8]

This biological toll on emotional suppression means that many Avoidant individuals face long-term physical health challenges, particularly those related to immune function and inflammatory responses. Silent stress doesn't stay silent forever. It lingers in the body, showing up as tension, fatigue, and sometimes illness, even when the mind insists everything is "fine." Over time, this hidden cost adds up, shaping not only your emotional world but your physical one too.

CHOREOGRAPHY OF THE SOLO TANGO

Let's look at the sophisticated emotional management Avoidants have developed. Your signature moves include specific strategies that help you navigate a world where closeness feels threatening:

Strategic Self-Sufficiency

This goes beyond basic independence. It's the art of making sure you NEVER need anyone for anything. Whether that's emotional support, practical help, or something else entirely. *I don't need help with this move. I'll just make four trips with my sedan instead of asking someone with a truck.*

Emotional Compartmentalization

The ability to neatly separate feelings from the rest of your experience, like organizing items into boxes that never touch. *I'm not upset about the breakup. That's in the relationship box, and I'm at work now.*

Idealization/Devaluation Shifting

Moving fluidly between seeing partners as perfect when they're distant and deeply flawed when they get close. *When we first met, he was amazing. Now I notice he laughs too loudly in restaurants.*

Subtle Boundary Expansion

Gradually increasing the psychological and physical space around you when intimacy grows, often so skillfully that others don't immediately notice. *I think I need to focus on this work project for the next few weeks.*

These aren't character flaws or manipulative tactics. They're adaptive strategies that once protected you and now limit you. They made sense in the environment where you first learned them. Recognizing them is the first step toward having choices beyond them. With awareness comes the power to choose something different. Even the smallest shift in how you respond can open the door to more connection and less fear.

ORIGINS OF AVOIDANT: BEYOND NEGLECT

Avoidant Attachment doesn't appear out of nowhere. It develops in environments where emotional needs are consistently:

- Dismissed ("Stop crying, it's not that bad.")
- Punished ("I'll give you something to cry about.")
- Ignored (parent physically present but emotionally absent)
- Overwhelmed by a caregiver's own needs ("Don't tell Dad about this, he's had a hard day.")

These experiences teach a powerful lesson: vulnerability leads to rejection, shame, or nothingness. Better to need nothing than to need and be disappointed.

Children are remarkably adaptable. When showing emotions doesn't work, when it consistently fails to create connection, they simply stop showing them. Not because they don't have feelings, but because expressing them doesn't help.

Over time, this adaptation becomes so automatic that many Avoidant adults genuinely don't register their emotional needs until they're at a breaking point. The inner voice that says, "I'm fine," grows so loud it drowns out the quieter voice whispering, "I'm lonely."

What often gets overlooked is that underneath the mask of self-sufficiency, the needs never actually disappear. They just go underground. That strategy may protect them from disappointment in the short term, but over the years it creates a gap between what they feel and what they allow themselves to express.

JAMIE'S DANCE: THE PERFECT CHILD

"Relationships just aren't a priority right now."

Jamie first came to me for career coaching, not relationship help. She was the picture of success. Executive position, stylish condo, global travels, and a wide circle of friends.

"I'm focused on my career," she explained with a confident smile.

It wasn't until our fourth session that Jamie's relationship patterns became clear. Every new man followed the same steps: an exciting beginning, a growing connection, and then an abrupt ending a few months later.

"It's like clockwork," she admitted. "Everything's great until I start getting busy at work and then they just need way too much. It's like every time I start dating, work just gets so busy! It's not my fault I have to work!" And yet as we worked together, I noticed that when she wasn't dating, she seemed fine to have a work-life balance. She had good friends, took trips, and did her self-care regimen religiously. Why all of a sudden, when there was a new relationship, did work become busier?

We started exploring her childhood. Jamie spoke proudly of her independence. Her father, a military officer, was deployed for months at a time. Her mother worked seventy-hour weeks as an attorney. By eight years old, Jamie was making her own meals and getting herself to school.

"My parents gave me everything I needed," she emphasized. "We weren't touchy-feely, but that made me strong."

What she couldn't see was how this environment had shaped her. When I asked who she went to with big feelings as a child, she looked genuinely confused. "You didn't bring problems to my parents," she said after a long pause. "They had real problems. Actual problems like important work, bills, adult stuff. Kid feelings weren't... relevant."

Jamie had learned **three** powerful lessons:

1. Emotional needs are an imposition on others.
2. Independence is not just valued but required.
3. The less you need, the more you're loved.

These lessons served her well in childhood. She became the perfect low-maintenance daughter, but this sabotaged her adult relationships. What kept her safe back then was now the very thing keeping her stuck. She'd been taught that needing nothing was the way to stay safe in a relationship.

Jamie danced the **Solo Tango** with every man because it was the only dance she was taught. She'd never experienced the vulnerable, messy back-and-forth of mutual dependence. Each time her relationships approached genuine vulnerability and intimacy, her internal alarm system blared: DANGER! RETREAT! PROTECT!

"Men just don't understand ambition," she'd tell me, rolling her eyes. "The minute I have to work late, they get all clingy, and it gives me the ick."

But the pattern was too consistent to ignore. Somehow, these "work emergencies" only appeared when relationships reached the two-ish month mark. Right when emotional intimacy started to deepen.

And like many with Avoidant Attachment, Jamie consistently found herself drawn to partners who challenged this pattern: emotionally expressive people who pursued connection openly. The very qualities that attracted her initially became overwhelming as relationships deepened.

Coach's Note: The Magnetic Pull of Opposites

There's a reason Avoidant and Anxious individuals often find each other: their opposing strategies create an initially compelling fit. The Anxious partner's expressive warmth melts through some of the Avoidant's defenses, while the Avoidant's self-sufficiency provides a sense of strength that the Anxious partner craves.

It's like a lock and key... until it isn't.

Eventually, the Anxious partner's need for reassurance triggers the Avoidant's need for space, creating a pursue-withdraw cycle that confirms both people's worst relationship fears. The Anxious partner thinks, *See? No one stays.* The Avoidant thinks, *See? Everyone demands too much.*

Research suggests these opposing Styles find each other at rates that are far higher than random chance would predict.[9] It's as if we subconsciously seek the very dynamic that will challenge our deepest Attachment Wounds.

FROM SOLO TO DUET

Here's the truth many Avoidant individuals never hear: your capacity for independence is a genuine strength. The problem isn't your self-sufficiency; it's that this strength has become your only strategy.

Secure Attachment isn't about surrendering your autonomy. It's about expanding your range: maintaining your cherished independence while creating space for chosen connection.

And here's the most important part: this expansion is absolutely possible. The brain's capacity for change (neuroplasticity) means that with consistent, intentional practice, you can develop new patterns of relating.[10]

In **Part Two** of this book, we'll explore specific strategies for this transformation. But for now, know this: the very qualities that make you a good soloist (strength, resilience, self-awareness) are also qualities that can make you an exceptional partner in a duet. You don't have to choose between independence and connection. The most fulfilling relationships honor both.

SPEAK HONEST: DANCING WITH MY WALLS

I didn't recognize my own Avoidant Attachment for a long time.

In fact, I thought I was just... independent. Driven. Strong. The kind of woman who didn't need anyone. I could build a business, raise a child, clean the entire house from top to bottom, and still have enough energy to avoid the hard conversations. That was my specialty: **productive avoidance.**

Back in my first marriage, this pattern was everywhere. We could be in the middle of an argument, and I'd be halfway to the door or already buried in work. Conflict made me want to run. Closeness made me claustrophobic. Intimacy made me itch.

But it didn't start with him. In high school, there was a sweet guy who really liked me. I liked him too. But his interest felt overwhelming. When he asked me to homecoming, I mumbled, "Yeah, I guess," and then spent the entire night hiding from him.

Poor guy. *(If you're reading this, I still owe you a dance, an apology... and probably therapy money.)* All he did was show up, and it sent me straight into shutdown.

That was my pattern. The ones who liked me? Too much. Too intense. The ones who didn't? I chased them like a moth to flame. It felt safer to want someone who didn't want me back. That way, I could stay in the dance without ever getting too close.

I carried this pattern into adulthood without even realizing it. I created distance in a thousand ways. I built a business and told myself I was "just busy." I skipped date nights to finish one more project. When my husband came home from work, I'd retreat to my office with my laptop, convinced that being productive somehow made me safe.

But behind the scenes, I was lonely. Even in a room full of people. Even in a marriage. I told myself that needing space meant I was strong. That saying "no" all the time made me powerful. But the truth is, I was **terrified** of letting anyone get too close.

I didn't see any of this clearly until I dated someone who was

Avoidant. Suddenly, I was the one reaching, overthinking, yearning for connection while he pulled away. And it hit me like a brick to the chest: this is what I've been doing. This is how I've made other people feel.

That moment cracked something open in me.

I started reading about Attachment Theory. I started asking questions. I stopped seeing my avoidance as a personality trait and started recognizing it as a protective strategy.

A brilliant one, actually. One that helped me survive, but one that was now keeping me from the kind of love I deeply wanted.

Yes, avoidance made me strong. But it also made me lonely *(like soul-crushingly lonely.)*

Learning about Attachment Theory changed everything for me. It helped me see that my independence, while valuable, had become a wall rather than a strength. True strength isn't found in isolation. It's found in the courage to stay present even when every instinct says RUN.

I still value my independence. That has not changed. But I have learned that connection does not mean losing myself. It can mean finding parts of me I never knew existed. When I stopped treating intimacy as a threat and started seeing it as a teacher, I realized that closeness could expand me, not shrink me. It asked me to bring more of me to the table, not less. And it reminded me that strength can look like staying present, even when my first impulse is to retreat.

That's what this whole book is about. Recognizing your old dance and learning a new one. One that makes room for connection without sacrificing who you are. Because listen, I'm still me. I still love alone time. I still love working. And yes, I still hate talking things out to death. But now, I don't have to choose between closeness and autonomy. I get both. And so do you.

YOUR TURN: SOLO TANGO REFLECTION QUESTIONS

1. When was the last time you felt the urge to create distance in a relationship that was going well? What specific thoughts or physical sensations came up?

2. Which Avoidant strategy is most familiar to you: Strategic Self-Sufficiency, Emotional Compartmentalization, Idealization/Devaluation Shifting, or Subtle Boundary Expansion?

3. What did your childhood environment teach you about expressing emotional needs? Were they welcomed, ignored, or discouraged?

4. What's one small step you could take toward letting someone get a little closer, even when your instinct is to pull away?

Remember, the goal isn't to become someone you're not. It's to reclaim parts of yourself that got lost in the necessary adaptations of childhood. Your independence is beautiful. But connection can be too.

You've mastered dancing alone. Perhaps it's time to discover what it feels like to dance together while still honoring your need for **space** and **autonomy**.

Three

PENDULUM SWING DANCE
DISORGANIZED ATTACHMENT

One moment you're desperate for closeness, the next you're terrified or disgusted by it.

I was doing it again.

Three days ago, I texted him a heartfelt message: "I miss you so much. Can't wait to see you this weekend."

Two days ago, I called him **twice**, leaving a rambling voicemail about how special our connection felt.

Yesterday, I spent hours planning our next date. Researching restaurants, making reservations, even buying a new outfit.

And today? Today I was crafting a carefully worded text explaining why I couldn't see him anymore.

My finger hovered over the send button as confusion clouded my mind. What was happening? I genuinely liked this guy. He had been nothing but kind, consistent, and interested. There were no red flags, no valid reasons to end things.

Yet here I was, suddenly overwhelmed by the certainty that I needed to get out. The same connection that had felt magical yesterday now felt suffocating. The same man who had seemed perfect was now, somehow, completely wrong.

A part of me was screaming: "Run! Protect yourself! He'll hurt you eventually!"

Another part was whispering: "What's wrong with you? He's amazing. Why can't you just be normal?"

I deleted the breakup text and threw my phone across the couch, burying my face in my hands. Why did I keep doing this? Why did I swing so wildly between desperate closeness and panicked distance? Why couldn't I just be... normal?

What I couldn't see then was that this wasn't about this man, or even about me being "crazy" *(though that's exactly how I felt).*

This was the **Pendulum Swing Dance** in action.

WELCOME TO DISORGANIZED ATTACHMENT

Let's talk about Disorganized Attachment. If you've ever felt simultaneously terrified of **abandonment** AND **engulfment**, if you've pursued someone intensely only to push them away once they responded, if your relationships feel like emotional whiplash... welcome to perhaps the most confusing club of all.

Disorganized Attachment (sometimes called Fearful-Avoidant Attachment) is characterized by contradictory, often chaotic approaches to relationships. Unlike Anxious Attachment (fear of abandonment) or Avoidant Attachment (fear of engulfment), Disorganized Attachment features both fears simultaneously. People with this Attachment Stance deeply crave connection but are equally terrified of it. The result? A relationship approach that can feel like you're constantly fighting yourself. *(Basically, it's an inner Fight Club with no audience and way too many rounds.)*

Which is exactly why I started calling Disorganized Attachment the **Pendulum Swing Dance**.

Picture a dance floor where a dancer is trying to perform two completely different routines at once. One moment, they're reaching out with passionate intensity, pulling their partner close and seeking maximum connection. The next, they're pushing away with equal force, creating distance and setting up walls.

This dancer isn't being manipulative or dramatic. They're responding to profound internal conflict. The same person who represents safety also represents danger. The same relationship that promises love also threatens pain.

Have you ever found yourself desperately seeking closeness with someone, only to feel trapped once you get it? Have you cycled through intense connection and sudden withdrawal, leaving both you and your partner emotionally **dizzy**? Have you thought, *I want you close... no wait, not that close... Actually wait... come back... don't leave me!* Within the span of hours or even minutes?

Congratulations, you're performing the Pendulum Swing Dance alongside approximately **7-10% of the population**.[1] That's millions of people trapped in a constant tug-of-war with themselves, wanting connection and fearing it in equal measure.

THE SCIENCE OF CONTRADICTION

To understand what's happening in Disorganized Attachment, we need to look at what happens when your nervous system faces an impossible dilemma: the same person who is supposed to be your **safe** haven is also the source of **fear** or danger.

Unlike the relatively straightforward patterns seen in Anxious or Avoidant Attachment, Disorganized Attachment involves a fundamental contradiction in the brain's approach to relationships. The pioneering work of Mary Main (who expanded on Ainsworth's Attachment categories) revealed something fascinating about children with Disorganized Attachment: their behavior didn't make logical sense.[2]

When stressed or frightened, these children would display bizarre, contradictory behaviors. For example, they would approach their caregiver but with their head turned away. Or they would **freeze** in place mid-movement or exhibit trance-like states. It was as if they couldn't decide whether to seek comfort or flee from danger.

Why? Because the Attachment system and the threat-response system were activated simultaneously, creating a neurobiological paradox. When the same person represents both safety and threat, the brain can't compute a coherent response.

This same paradox continues into adulthood. Brain imaging studies show that adults with Disorganized Attachment often display unusual activity patterns when thinking about close relationships.[3] Both approach-related and avoidance-related neural circuits activate at once, creating internal confusion that can feel overwhelming.

Dr. Bessel van der Kolk, trauma expert and author of *The Body Keeps the Score,* explains that this conflicted neural activity often stems from relationships where "the caregiver is both the source of and the solution to the child's distress."[4] The brain develops a fundamental ambivalence about closeness that persists into adult relationships.

THE PHYSICAL SYMPTOMS OF CHAOS

Disorganized Attachment doesn't just happen in your mind. It creates chaos in your body too. When you're caught in the Disorganized Dance, your nervous system gets trapped in a state that polyvagal theory researcher Dr. Stephen Porges calls "oscillating dysregulation."[5] Your body rapidly cycles between:

- **Sympathetic activation** (fight/flight): heart racing, breathing shallow, muscles tense—the physical state of anxiety and urgency that says: *pursue connection now!*

- **Dorsal vagal shutdown** (freeze/collapse): energy draining, mind going blank, feeling numb or distant—the physical state of withdrawal that says: *connection is dangerous, shut down!*

This physiological rollercoaster is exhausting. Your body never fully settles into either state long enough to resolve it, creating a chronic stress response that can manifest as:

- Digestive issues that flare up during relationship stress.
- Sleep disturbances that worsen during periods of intimacy.
- Mysterious physical symptoms that doctors can't diagnose.
- Chronic fatigue that no amount of rest seems to resolve.
- Immune weakness that makes you more susceptible to illness.

Research from the field of psychoneuroimmunology (the study of how psychology affects our immune system) has found that this type of Attachment-related stress takes a particularly heavy toll on physical health.[6] The constant state of internal conflict creates inflammatory responses, hormonal imbalances, and nervous system dysregulation that affect virtually every system in your body.

Your body literally cannot decide whether to move toward or away from connection, and this indecision becomes physically **painful** over time.

CHOREOGRAPHY OF THE PENDULUM SWING DANCE

So how do you know if you're dancing the Pendulum Swing? It is the push-pull pattern, the come-here-go-away rhythm that keeps you guessing. One moment you're desperate for closeness, the next you're terrified or disgusted by it. Let's break down the signature moves:

The Desperate Pursuit
One moment, you're all in. Texting constantly, planning future events, feeling an almost urgent need to secure the connection. *I've never felt this way about anyone. We have such an amazing connection. I think about you constantly.*

The Sudden Retreat
Then, often after achieving the closeness you sought, you feel smothered and need immediate distance. You might ghost, pick fights, or create barriers seemingly out of nowhere. *I need space. I'm not sure this is working. I don't think I can give you what you want.*

The Emotional Translator
You frequently misinterpret your partner's words and actions, viewing neutral statements through a lens of either abandonment or control. *You're busy on Friday? Clearly, you don't want to see me. You want to meet my friends? Why are you pressuring me?*

The Relationship Amnesia

Your feelings about your partner can completely transform over-night, making you question everything. Yesterday's "perfect match" becomes today's "obviously wrong person," with little middle ground. *I don't know what I was thinking. We're clearly incompatible.*

These aren't just random behaviors. These are your nervous system's **desperate** attempts to navigate an impossible situation: wanting closeness from the very thing that triggers your deepest fears. The pendulum swings as you try to find a safe emotional distance, but there isn't one, because the conflict is internal.

ORIGINS OF DISORGANIZED: BEYOND CHAOS

The roots of Disorganized Attachment run deeper and often darker than those of other Adapted Attachment Stances. While Anxious and Avoidant Attachment Stances typically develop from inconsistent or emotionally unavailable caregiving, Disorganized Attachment often stems from experiences when caregivers were:

- Frightening (unpredictable, threatening, or abusive)
- Frightened (themselves visibly terrified or overwhelmed)
- Dissociated (psychologically absent while physically present)
- Contradictory (mixed messages about safety and danger)

Dr. Judith Herman, trauma specialist and author of *Trauma and Recovery*, explains that Disorganized Attachment often develops when a child faces "the fundamental contradiction between the need to attach and the need to protect oneself."[7] When the caregiver is both the comfort and the threat, the child is left in an impossible position, unable to form a stable sense of security.

What makes this especially confusing is that the harmful behaviors weren't always there. Many people with Disorganized Attachment grew up with caregivers who could be warm, loving, and attentive one moment: then frightening, neglectful, or even harmful the next. This mix creates powerful bonds of love right alongside experiences of fear and helplessness, leaving the child torn between reaching for closeness and pulling away for safety.

This **intermittent reinforcement**, occasional nurturing mixed with unpredictability or danger, creates the strongest and most resistant-to-change Attachment bonds. It's the psychological equivalent of a gambling addiction: the occasional "win" keeps you coming back for more despite consistent losses.

Over time, the developing brain internalizes a profound mixed message: *I need connection to survive, but connection is dangerous.* This contradictory belief doesn't just affect how you relate to others. It also creates a divided relationship with yourself.

Imagine being a child and never knowing which version of your caregiver will show up. It's like stepping onto the dance floor blindfolded. Sometimes you're swept into a waltz of warmth, other times you're shoved into a tango of terror. That unpredictability wires your nervous system to stay on high alert, scanning constantly for danger even in moments of love.

MIA'S DANCE: THE CHAOTIC PARTNER

"It's like I'm two different people."

Mia came to me after her fourth breakup in two years. Each relationship had followed an almost identical pattern: intense connection, growing closeness, then a sudden urge to end things, followed by desperate attempts to reconcile once the breakup was final.

"When I'm single, all I want is a relationship. The minute I get one, I start looking for the exit," she explained to me during our first session.

Her most recent relationship with Jason brought this into painful focus. They met through friends and connected instantly. The first month was magical: deep conversations, passionate intimacy, constant communication. Mia was sure this time was different.

Then one evening, as they were planning a weekend trip, Jason casually mentioned, "My parents are excited to meet you when they visit next month."

Mia's chest tightened. By the time she got home, she was convinced the relationship was moving way too fast. She ended things by text, blocked his number, and felt relief for three days.

The relief eventually turned to panic. She begged him to take her back, and he agreed because he really did like her and wanted to make it work. Ironically, that was the exact reason she kept swinging. The more he wanted her, the more it scared her. Two weeks later, she ended things again. This time it was because he didn't respond quickly enough to a text, which she interpreted as rejection.

"I know I sound crazy," she told me, tears streaming down her face.

"I don't understand what's happening. I want a relationship more than anything, but as soon as I get close to someone, I either find reasons they're wrong for me or become convinced they're going to leave."

As we explored her history, a clearer picture emerged. Her father, while loving in many ways, struggled with alcoholism. When sober, he was attentive and affectionate. When drinking, he was unpredictable and frightening. Her mother, overwhelmed, often checked out emotionally.

This childhood environment taught Mia **three** contradictory lessons:

1. Love can transform into fear without warning.
2. Neither connection nor distance feels safe.
3. Closeness is both desperately needed yet feels dangerous.

These lessons created the perfect conditions for the **Pendulum Swing Dance** in her adult relationships. Mia craved the connection she'd experienced with her father's loving side while simultaneously fearing the hurt associated with his unpredictable side. Every relationship became a reenactment of this primary Attachment drama. It was as if she was forever bracing for the next step, never able to fully relax into the rhythm.

And like many with Disorganized Attachment, Mia had unconsciously developed an exquisite sensitivity to **emotional** cues. The slightest hint of either too much closeness or potential abandonment could trigger massive defensive reactions that confused both her and her partners.

Coach's Note: The Self-Fulfilling Prophecy

One of the cruelest aspects of Disorganized Attachment is how often it creates the very pain it's trying to avoid. Mia's fear of abandonment led her to push partners away before they could leave her, which ultimately resulted in *(you guess it!)*... being left. Her fear of being controlled led her to act unpredictably, which often prompted partners to become more controlling in their attempts to understand what was happening.

This self-fulfilling aspect creates a particularly vicious cycle. Each relationship that ends painfully **reinforces** the belief that relationships are both essential and dangerous, strengthening the Disorganized pattern.

For someone living this cycle, it doesn't feel like self-sabotage. It feels like survival. The nervous system is simply doing its best to avoid danger, even if that danger is only imagined. What looks from the outside like "mixed signals" is, on the inside, a desperate attempt to stay safe in a world that feels unpredictable.

Research by Dr. Amir Levine shows that this pattern can become so entrenched that people with Disorganized Attachment often dismiss or push away secure partners who could actually help break the cycle.[8] The unfamiliar experience of stable connection can feel more threatening than the familiar pain of chaotic relationships.

FROM SWINGING TO FLOWING

Here's the true hope in all of this: Disorganized Attachment may be the most painful Attachment pattern, but it also has tremendous potential for transformation. Why? Because the internal conflict at its core creates a natural impetus for change.

Dr. Daniel Siegel, psychiatrist and pioneer in the field of interpersonal neurobiology, uses the term "integration" to describe the process of bringing contradictory parts of ourselves into coherent relationship.[9] For someone with Disorganized Attachment, **integration** means developing the capacity to hold both the desire for connection and the fear of hurt without being torn apart by their opposition.

The key isn't to eliminate either the longing or the fear; it's to create enough internal stability that you can experience both without being controlled by either.

In **Part Two** of this book, we'll explore specific strategies for this integration. But for now, know this: the very sensitivity that makes Disorganized Attachment so painful can become your greatest strength. People who heal Disorganized Attachment often develop exceptional emotional intelligence, profound empathy, and a rare capacity for authentic connection. Trust me on this one, I've not only studied this dance, I've also performed every chaotic step of it and somehow managed to choreograph a whole new routine on the other side.

Your pendulum doesn't have to keep swinging to extremes. With practice and support, you can find a centered flow that honors both your need for connection and your need for safety.

SPEAK HONEST: DANCING WITH MY CHAOS

When I first discovered Disorganized Attachment, it felt like someone had been secretly recording my relationship history and turned it into a psychological theory.

The pattern was undeniable: intense connection followed by sudden panic, desperate clinging followed by cold withdrawal, loving someone deeply while simultaneously pushing them away. I'd lived this contradiction my entire adult life without understanding why.

In my first marriage, the Pendulum Swing was at its most destructive. I'd crave closeness from my then-husband, pursue it relentlessly, then feel trapped the moment I received it. I'd push him away with harsh words or emotional walls, then panic at the distance I'd created and start the cycle again. Looking back with compassion now, I can see that I became emotionally abusive in that relationship. Not because I was a bad person, but because I was caught in a Disorganized Attachment pattern, I had no tools to recognize or manage.

After my divorce, I entered a relationship that triggered the most intense Disorganized Attachment I'd ever experienced. I was utterly convinced this man was my soulmate. Yet once we were finally together, I'd find myself Googling "am I settling?" at 2 a.m. while he slept beside me. I'd cry myself to sleep when he didn't text goodnight, then feel smothered and pull away when he showed consistent attention.

Even in my current relationship *(with the man I now call my husband… and occasionally my emotional-support snack fairy)*, the pattern emerged. Early in our relationship, right after we'd made things official, I felt a sudden, overwhelming certainty that I needed to end things. Nothing had happened to trigger this feeling. He was kind, consistent, and caring. But the closer we got, the more my internal alarm system blared: **DANGER!**

The most maddening aspect of the Pendulum Swing Dance is being fully aware of the contradictions while feeling powerless to stop them. I'd catch myself sabotaging relationships in real time, watching my behavior as if from outside my body, screaming internally at myself to stop while simultaneously unable to change course. It was like having two opposing selves sharing one mind. One desperate for connection, the other terrified by it.

The physical symptoms were unbearable at times. When intimacy increased, I'd experience **crushing** chest pain, racing thoughts, and an overwhelming urge to flee. My body would enter fight-or-flight mode at precisely the moments when I was receiving the love I claimed to want.

During one particularly tender moment with my partner, I excused myself to the bathroom where I dry-heaved from anxiety. All because he kissed me. If I told this story to friends, they'd immediately advise me to end the relationship, "Your body is telling you something!" But that well-meaning advice misses the point entirely. My reaction wasn't about him or anything he did wrong. It was my nervous system's programmed response to **vulnerability**, a physiological alarm triggered by the very closeness I consciously desired.

This is what makes healing Disorganized Attachment so challenging. Conventional relationship wisdom doesn't apply. The problem isn't your partner or even the relationship itself; it's the conflict between your yearning for connection and your fear of it. Understanding this contradiction was my first step toward healing. I had to accept that my reactions weren't reliable indicators of compatibility or love. They were echoes of earlier Attachment Wounds in need of compassion and care.

The path forward wasn't about finding the "right" person who wouldn't trigger these responses. It was about building a relationship with myself where I could observe my reactions without judgment, self-soothe through the panic, and gradually rewire my association between intimacy and danger. Only then could I begin to experience love without also fighting to escape it.

YOUR TURN: PENDULUM SWING DANCE REFLECTION QUESTIONS

1. Think about your most chaotic relationship. Can you identify moments when you swung rapidly between craving closeness and needing distance? What triggered these swings?

2. Which feels more frightening to you: the possibility of being abandoned, or the possibility of being controlled?

3. When you feel yourself starting to swing from one extreme to another in a relationship, what physical sensations do you notice in your body?

4. Can you identify patterns from your early relationships that might have taught you that connection is both essential and dangerous?

Remember, Disorganized Attachment isn't a character flaw; it's an adaptation that helped you survive contradictory experiences of love. The very fact that you can recognize these patterns means you've already begun the journey toward integration.

You may have mastered the Pendulum Swing Dance, but sweetheart, you don't have to keep dancing until you're dizzy. A steadier, more integrated rhythm is waiting for you.

In Part Two, we'll begin looking at how to shift these patterns and create the kind of love that feels steady instead of chaotic. You'll learn how to calm your nervous system, how to soothe the panic when it rises, and how to build a sense of safety inside yourself that carries into your relationships.

For now, pause and give yourself credit. Naming the dance and seeing the steps clearly means you are no longer caught inside of it. That awareness is powerful. It's the beginning of choosing differently, and it opens the door to love that feels safe, steady, and free.

And if you're feeling a little weighed down after exploring all of these Nonsecure Attachment Stances, keep reading. What comes next is a picture of what Secure connection can look like. A rhythm that shows you where you're headed.

Four

SMOOTH WALTZ
SECURE ATTACHMENT

Two dancers move together in perfect harmony, yet each maintains their own balance and presence.

I watched her from across the restaurant, this woman who was completely unknown to me except for one unmistakable quality. The ease with which she existed in her relationship.

She and her partner were having dinner at the table next to mine. Nothing about their interaction was particularly dramatic or even noteworthy. There were no grand gestures, no excessive displays of affection. Just a quiet, steady flow of **connection** interspersed with comfortable silences.

When her partner excused himself to take a call, she didn't anxiously check her phone or scan the room. She simply sipped her wine and enjoyed the moment. When he returned and mentioned the call was work-related and might cut their evening short, she didn't stiffen with rejection or cling with desperation. She nodded with understanding, squeezed his hand, and suggested they enjoy their time together now.

It was their ease that fascinated me. The way they moved toward and away from each other without drama or threat. The way they could express their needs directly. The way they seemed to trust both the connection and themselves.

I remember thinking, *Is this even possible? Can relationships really feel this... **uncomplicated**?*

At that point in my life, locked in the tumultuous patterns I've described in previous chapters, this kind of interaction seemed as foreign to me as speaking a language I'd never learned.

What I was witnessing was the Smooth Waltz of Secure Attachment. And yes, it is possible, even if it was never taught to you.

WELCOME TO SECURE ATTACHMENT

Let's talk about **Secure Attachment**. If you've read the previous chapters, you might be thinking, *Finally! Something positive!* And you're right, Secure Attachment is the goal we're working toward. The healthier pattern that makes relationships both nourishing and stable.

This Attachment Stance is characterized by a fundamental trust in relationships. A deep-seated belief that you are worthy of love and that others can be relied upon. People with Secure Attachment generally have a positive view of themselves and others. They're comfortable with both intimacy and independence, and they don't view these states as contradictory.

That's why I call Secure Attachment the **Smooth Waltz**.

Picture a classic waltz, where two dancers move together in perfect harmony, yet each maintains their own balance and presence. They draw close, they create space, they respond to subtle cues from each other, all while maintaining a steady rhythm. The dance is neither clingy nor distant—it's fluid, responsive, and grounded.

Dancing the **Smooth Waltz** doesn't mean your relationship is perfect or that you never face challenges. Rather, it means you have the emotional tools to navigate those challenges without your Attachment Stance going into crisis mode. You trust that disagreements don't threaten the relationship, that temporary distance doesn't mean abandonment, and that vulnerability doesn't lead to exploitation.

Have you ever found yourself able to express a need directly, without excessive anxiety or elaborate strategies? Have you ever felt disappointed by a partner but discussed it calmly rather than spiraling? Have you experienced the profound relief of being exactly who you are in a relationship and feeling accepted for it?

If so, you've had moments of dancing the Smooth Waltz, even if it's not your predominant pattern yet. And the good news is that approximately **50-55% of the population**[1] has this Attachment Stance, showing us it's both common and achievable.

THE SCIENCE OF SECURITY

Secure Attachment looks very different on the inside. The brain and body respond in ways that are strikingly unlike the patterns we've seen in earlier chapters.

Research using neuroimaging techniques shows that individuals with Secure Attachment process relationship information differently.[2] When faced with difficult relationship challenges, their brains don't automatically activate threat responses. Instead, their prefrontal cortex, *(the part of the brain that stops you from doing dumb shit)* stays actively engaged, allowing for thoughtful responses rather than emotionally reactive ones.

Remember Dr. Daniel Siegel and his description of integration from the previous chapter? It's relevant here as well; he describes this as the ability to process emotional information without becoming overwhelmed or shutting down. This integration allows Securely Attached people to remain present and responsive even when they're in the middle of relationship stress.

Physiologically, Secure Attachment is linked with a more balanced autonomic nervous system. Dr. Stephen Porges' Polyvagal Theory helps us understand why: Secure Attachment promotes what he calls a "ventral vagal state," a condition of calm, open engagement.[3] In this state, your body isn't preoccupied with fighting danger or withdrawing from threat. It's optimized for connection, creativity, and well-being.

This neurophysiological security creates a remarkable feedback loop. Because Securely Attached individuals aren't constantly scanning for relationship threats, they have more cognitive and emotional resources available for positive engagement. This leads to more rewarding interactions, which reinforce the belief that relationships are safe and valuable, further strengthening Secure Attachment patterns.

THE PHYSICAL BENEFITS OF SAFETY

Secure Attachment doesn't just appear in brain scans; it shows up throughout the body as a dynamic state of regulated flow.

When you're dancing the Smooth Waltz, your body exists in what trauma expert Dr. Bessel van der Kolk calls your "optimal arousal zone."[4] Neither hyperactivated with **anxiety** nor numbed with **avoidance**. You can feel deeply without being overwhelmed. You can process emotions without being consumed by them.

Research in psychoneuroimmunology (the study of how psychology affects our immune system) has found some remarkable benefits associated with Secure Attachment:

- Improved immunity and inflammatory responses.[5]
- Better cardiovascular health and lower blood pressure.[6]
- More efficient stress recovery and lower cortisol levels.[7]
- Better sleep quality and more consistent energy levels.[8]

These physiological advantages don't mean Securely Attached people never experience stress—they absolutely do. The difference is in the recovery. Their bodies return to baseline more quickly after upset, and they're less likely to remain in prolonged states of fight, flight, or freeze.

The ability to regulate the body's stress response directly supports our emotional regulation. Dr. Sue Johnson (the creator of Emotionally Focused Therapy) reminds us that emotional balance is a team sport.[9] Secure Attachment creates the kind of partnership where that balance can thrive.

CHOREOGRAPHY OF THE SMOOTH WALTZ

So, what does Secure Attachment realistically look like in practice? Let's break down the signature moves you'll want to notice and practice yourself:

The Direct Expression

The ability to state needs and feelings clearly, without excessive apology, manipulation, or suppression. *I'm feeling overwhelmed with work this week and could use some extra support.*

The Flexible Distance

Moving toward and away from your partner with ease and transparency, respecting both connection and autonomy as natural rhythms. *I'd love some time to myself this morning, and I'm looking forward to our dinner tonight.*

The Repair Response

Addressing ruptures in the relationship promptly and constructively, focusing on resolution rather than punishment or withdrawal. *I didn't handle that well earlier. Can we talk about what happened?*

The Empathic Attunement

Remaining present with your partner's experience without taking it personally or becoming defensive, even when it's challenging. *I can see why you were hurt by what I said. That makes sense.*

These moves reflect what Attachment researcher Dr. Mary Main discovered when studying Secure Attachment patterns: Secure individuals have access to a coherent narrative about their relationships.[10] They can talk about both **positive** and **negative** experiences in an integrated way, without minimizing difficult emotions or becoming overwhelmed by them.

ORIGINS OF SECURE: BEYOND PERFECTION

When discussing the origins of the Smooth Waltz, there's a common misconception that it requires perfect, flawless parenting. The research tells a different, more hopeful story.

What creates Secure Attachment isn't perfection, it's **repair and consistency**. Dr. Ed Tronick's famous "Still Face Experiment"[11] demonstrated that all parent-child interactions include moments of disconnection. What distinguishes healthy relationships is not the absence of these ruptures but the consistent repair that follows.

The research is quite liberating for parents: Tronick's studies found that even in healthy relationships, parents and children are in perfect attunement only about 30% of the time.[12] This means you don't need to get it right all the time, **just enough of the time**. This concept is often called "good enough parenting," a term coined by pediatrician and psychoanalyst Dr. Donald Winnicott.[13] The child doesn't need perfection; they need a caregiver who is emotionally present and responsive more often than not.

Secure Attachment typically develops when a child experiences caregivers who are:

- Emotionally available a majority—not all—of the time.
- Responsive to distress in a timely and appropriate manner.
- Consistent in their reactions, creating predictability.
- Capable of repairing moments of disconnection.
- Supportive of both connection and independence.

This understanding gives us an important insight: Secure Attachment isn't about never making mistakes or never feeling negative emotions. It's about having the confidence that disconnections can be repaired and that the relationship will withstand both intimacy and separateness.

OLIVIA'S DANCE: THE CONNECTION SEEKER

When Olivia first came to my coaching practice, she wasn't experiencing deep Attachment Wounds or severe relationship distress. She was simply noticing a pattern: despite having a relatively secure foundation, she kept finding herself with emotionally unavailable partners.

"I have good relationships with my family," she explained during our first session. "My parents were loving and generally responsive. I don't have abandonment issues or fear intimacy. So why do I keep ending up with people who can't fully show up emotionally?"

Olivia's childhood had indeed provided her with the roots of a Secure foundation. Her parents were attuned to her needs about a third of the time, which research shows is sufficient. They were usually consistent, repaired ruptures, and created a stable home environment.

Yet Olivia had absorbed **subtle** messages about emotional expression. "My parents loved me, but they weren't particularly comfortable with big feelings," she reflected. "When I was upset, they'd comfort me physically but rarely helped me navigate the emotions themselves. It wasn't that feelings were bad; they just weren't discussed or explored much."

This pattern created a blind spot in Olivia's relationship radar. While she could form Secure connections and wasn't afraid of intimacy in general, she had unconsciously learned to accept emotional unavailability as normal. She wasn't drawn to these partners out of insecurity but out of familiarity. This was the emotional temperature she knew. Because it didn't feel unsafe, Olivia never questioned it, even though deep down she sensed something was missing from her relationships.

Our work together focused not just on healing Attachment Wounds but on raising her awareness of her Attachment Needs and recognizing when these needs weren't being met. She began:

- Noticing when she minimized her need for connection.
- Spotting early signs of emotional unavailability in partners.
- Having direct talks about emotions and needs.
- Setting standards for the intimacy she wanted.

Six months into our work, Olivia met Jordan, someone who matched her natural secure tendencies but who was also comfortable with emotional depth and expressiveness.

"It feels different," she told me, clearly surprised. "When I express a need, Jordan doesn't get defensive or pull away. When we disagree, we actually talk about it instead of sweeping it under the rug. It's like... we're on the same team."

Olivia's story illustrates an important point: even people with relatively Secure Attachment can benefit from becoming more conscious of their patterns and needs. The foundation was there; she just needed to build upon it by recognizing and requesting the level of **emotional connection** she truly desired.

This gradual refinement of what we want and need in relationships is part of the ongoing Attachment journey for everyone, regardless of our starting point. Growth doesn't always come from fixing what is broken. Sometimes it comes from daring to want more, to ask for deeper connection, and to no longer settle for almost good enough.

Coach's Note: Earned Security

One of the most hopeful discoveries in Attachment research is the concept of Earned Secure Attachment.[14] This term, developed by Dr. Mary Main and her colleagues, describes individuals who didn't experience Secure Attachment in childhood but developed it later through other relationships and experiences.

Studies suggest that roughly 20-30% of people with Secure Attachment began with insecure patterns and developed security over time.[15] This transformation typically occurs through:

- Supportive, consistent relationships (romantic partnerships, close friendships, therapeutic or coaching relationships).

- Taking time to reflect on the past and make sense of those experiences.

- New emotional experiences that directly contradict old Attachment expectations.

- Deliberate practice of Secure behaviors, even before they feel natural.

This research offers profound hope: your Attachment Stance is not fixed by your childhood. The brain remains plastic, capable of forming new neural pathways based on new experiences. The beauty of Earned Secure Attachment is that healing is always possible. Each new safe connection lays down fresh pathways in the brain. Over time, those pathways can reshape how you experience love and closeness.

FROM SCATTERED TO SMOOTH

If you've identified with the Anxious, Avoidant, or Disorganized patterns described in previous chapters, you might be wondering, *Can I develop Secure Attachment?* The answer is a resounding **yes**.

Developing Secure Attachment as an adult is like learning a new dance when you've spent years performing different steps. It feels awkward at first. Your muscle memory pulls you back to familiar moves. But with practice and the right guidance, the new patterns gradually become more natural.

The journey toward the **Smooth Waltz** is deeply personal, and it looks different for everyone. For some, it involves healing childhood wounds and reprocessing early experiences. For others, it's about challenging the belief that they're needy. And for others, it will be learning how to set healthy boundaries. The end goal is the same: learning and practicing new ways of connecting that weren't modeled for us growing up.

What's universal is that this journey requires both **awareness** and **action**. Simply understanding your Attachment Stance isn't enough to change it, though it's a crucial first step. Real transformation happens through new experiences that show your nervous system, not just your mind, that different ways of relating are possible.

This might mean taking risks to express needs you've always hidden. It might mean setting boundaries when you'd normally people-please. It might mean staying present with uncomfortable emotions rather than running from them or drowning in them. Whatever form it takes, each new experience creates a template for what's possible in relationships.

In **Part Two** of this book, we'll explore practical tools and strategies for this journey. But for now, know this: the Smooth Waltz is learnable, even if it wasn't your first dance. I've witnessed this transformation in hundreds of clients and experienced it myself. The steps may feel unfamiliar at first, but with practice, they become your new normal.

SPEAK HONEST: DANCING WITH MY NEW RHYTHM

Secure Attachment wasn't exactly the vibe in my house. *(Imagine the chaos of musical chairs, but the music never stopped.)* As I've shared in previous chapters, my early childhood experiences created templates for Anxious pursuit, Avoidant withdrawal, and Disorganized confusion. Not for the steady rhythm of the Smooth Waltz.

Learning this new dance has been a journey of both small steps and significant leaps. I remember the first time I expressed a need directly to my current husband without apologizing, catastrophizing, or cushioning it with a hundred qualifiers. My heart was racing. My body was braced for rejection or conflict. I was ready to either **fight** for the need or **dismiss** it as unimportant, depending on his response.

Instead, he simply said, "Thanks for telling me. That makes sense." *(Wait what?! Where's the gaslighting and the blaming?!)*

The simplicity of the exchange shocked me. Was it really possible for relationships to work this way? Could needs be expressed and met without drama? Could conflicts be addressed without someone being abandoned or controlled?

Each positive experience created a tiny crack in my old Attachment beliefs. Each **repair** after a disagreement proved that ruptures didn't have to end relationships. Each time I set a boundary, and it was respected, my nervous system recorded: *it's safe to be authentic.*

The most profound shift came when I realized that Secure Attachment isn't about finding a perfect partner who never triggers your insecurities. It's about developing the internal resources to navigate those triggers when they inevitably arise.

I still have moments of Attachment activation, times when an old fear of abandonment or engulfment surfaces. The difference is that now I can name it, sit with it, and **choose** my response rather than being controlled by the automatic reaction. I can tell my partner, "I'm feeling that old anxiety spike, and I know it's not about you," instead of either clinging to him or pushing him away.

This capacity to observe my Attachment patterns without being consumed by them is what Dr. Kristin Neff would call self-compassion.[16] Which is the ability to witness your own struggles with kindness rather than judgment. It's this compassionate awareness that creates space for new choices, even when old patterns are activated.

The Smooth Waltz isn't about never stepping on toes or never missing a beat. It's about the capacity to recover, adjust, and keep dancing with both grace and authenticity. It's about **trusting** yourself and your partner enough to stay present through both harmony and discord.

And this kind of secure connection isn't just nice to have... it's transformative. Research consistently shows that Secure relationships are a primary determinant of overall well-being, affecting everything from physical health to professional success to emotional resilience.

As Dr. Sue Johnson eloquently puts it, "We are born to connect. It's our primary motivating force in life." When we dance the **Smooth Waltz**, we're not just creating better relationships, we're fulfilling our deepest human potential.

YOUR TURN: SMOOTH WALTZ REFLECTION QUESTIONS

1. Think of a time you felt truly safe and supported in a relationship. What about that experience made you feel secure?

2. How do you know when you're balanced between closeness and independence? What does that feel like in your body?

3. In what ways do you already show up as a secure partner, friend, or family member?

4. What's one small daily action you can take to build more trust, steadiness, or openness in your current relationships?

Because let's be honest. Girl, you must be so tired of doing the same dumb shit in relationships. The drama, the overthinking, the chasing, the pushing away... it's exhausting. And if you want to heal as badly as I think you might *(otherwise, why did you pick up this book, to just improve your small talk skills??)*, then keep reading.

Part Two is about rewiring your rhythm so you don't just **KNOW** better, you actually **DO** better. This is where we turn up the volume, slip on those fancy dancing shoes, and finally learn the dance that was always meant for you.

PART TWO

Rewire Your Rhythm

"One can ascend to a higher development only by bringing rhythm and repetition into one's life. Rhythm holds sway in all nature"
- Rudolf Steiner

BEFORE WE HEAL

So... did you recognize your choreography?

Those steps you've been dancing your whole life without realizing you learned them somewhere, from someone, for reasons that made perfect sense at the time? Maybe you cringed a little. Maybe you felt seen. Maybe you wanted to text your ex and say, "SEE! THIS IS WHY WE DIDN'T WORK."

(Please don't do that. Save the screenshots for your group chat like the rest of us.)

Here's what happens after you recognize your dance: you either want to change everything immediately, or you want to give up because it feels too hard. Both reactions are totally normal. Both are also not particularly helpful.

If you're in the "fix me now" camp, I get it. You've spent so many years wondering why love feels complicated, and now you have answers. You want to reprogram your nervous system like updating software and be done with it. But neuroscience tells us that your brain needs **repetition**, not just recognition.

Lasting change happens through repetition plus emotional experience. Your brain literally needs to practice new patterns over and over *(and over)* again before they become automatic. And yes, it can feel painfully slow at times, like taking two steps forward and one step back. But those steps still count. They're still progress.

If you're in the "this is hopeless" camp, I see you too. Maybe reading about your Attachment Stance felt like getting a diagnosis for something you can't cure. Maybe you're thinking, *Great, so I'm broken and too messed up to do anything about it.*

Trauma research shows us that these patterns aren't personality defects or character flaws. They're brilliant adaptations your nervous system created to keep you safe. Your brain can unlearn these patterns and create new ones through patience, practice, and self-compassion.

The same way repetition carved those old patterns, repetition can also create new ones. Every time you pause instead of react, every time you notice your triggers without shaming yourself, every time you choose a new step in the dance, you are slowly rewiring. Healing is not about erasing the past, it is about teaching your nervous system that safety and connection are possible now. The truth is you don't need to become someone else to earn love. You are already enough as you are, and the work ahead is simply helping your brain and body believe that truth in real time.

Part Two isn't going to magically transform you into a Secure Attachment goddess overnight. You're not going to read Chapter Five and suddenly stop spiraling when he doesn't text back. You're not going to finish Chapter Eight and never feel the urge to run when someone gets too close. What you will start to notice is that those spirals don't last as long, those urges soften, and the old dance loses its grip a little at a time. That's the work. That's the path.

Here's what you ARE going to do, you're going to learn how to **D.A.N.C.E.**

D ISCOVER YOUR ATTACHMENT STANCE

And I mean really discover it, not just take a quiz and call it a day. We're talking about recognizing your patterns in real time, understanding your triggers, and seeing how your style shows up differently with different people.

A LLEVIATE YOUR ATTACHMENT WOUNDS

Those deep beliefs about your worthiness, safety, and lovability that keep you stuck in old patterns. We're going to challenge them with compassion and evidence.

N URTURE YOUR ATTACHMENT NEEDS

Because you're not "too much" or "too needy." You're human. And humans have needs. We're going to help you honor yours without apology.

C OMMUNICATE WITH CONFIDENCE

The skills to express your needs, set boundaries, and navigate conflict without losing yourself or your partner in the process.

E MBODY SECURE ATTACHMENT

This is where all your hard work comes together, and you learn a new way of being in relationships. You won't be perfect, but you will be present. Not fearless, but brave.

This isn't going to be the type of dance where you follow someone else's lead and hope you don't trip. It's the kind where you know your own rhythm, trust your own steps, and can dance with a partner without losing yourself in the process. The kind where if you step on each other's toes, you both laugh and turn it into part of the choreography instead of evidence that you're doing everything wrong.

Your old dance steps had a purpose. They served you well, protecting you when safety felt scarce. But you don't have to keep dancing those same patterns forever. You've outgrown survival mode, and now you get to create something more—something steady, more nourishing, and more alive.

You're ready for a new rhythm, one that feels like home instead of fear. A dance where closeness feels safe, where love doesn't mean losing yourself, and where joy belongs in every step.

So, let's begin.

Let's learn how to **dance like no one's leaving**.

Five

DISCOVER YOUR ATTACHMENT STANCE

Needing help isn't a sign of weakness.
It's a sign of wisdom.

Sarah came to our first coaching call convinced she had herself all figured out.

"I have Disorganized Attachment," she announced with the confidence of someone who'd just solved a complex puzzle. "I took the quiz on your website, and it said Disorganized. Which makes total sense. I'm clingy and needy with my boyfriend, Marcus, but then sometimes I want space. That's the **push-pull thing**, right? So obviously this is me."

I could hear the frustration in her voice, like she was confessing to having some kind of relationship disease.

"Tell me more about wanting space," I explored.

"Well, like last weekend, Marcus wanted to spend the entire Saturday together, and I was like, 'Can I just have a few hours to myself to read?' And then I felt terrible about it because I know I'm supposed to want to be with him all the time if I really love him. But sometimes I just... need a break. That's the Disorganized part. I want him close, but then I push him away."

"Where did you learn that wanting alone time means you don't love someone?" I asked.

Sarah paused, her shoulders lifted in a half-shrug as she spoke, as though she wasn't sure if she was making a statement or asking for reassurance. "I... I don't know. I guess... I mean, I just always thought that if you really love someone, you want to be with them all the time."

"And what do you think pushing someone away actually looks like?"

Another pause. "Well... I guess it would be more like... avoiding them? Not communicating? Maybe leaving without explanation?"

"So how would you describe what you did with Marcus?"

"I... I asked for what I needed?" Sarah's voice had a question mark at the end, like she was testing out a new idea. This was the first time she'd considered that asking directly wasn't pushing away but actually leaning in.

"What else do you notice about how you handled that situation?"

"I was honest with him. I didn't just disappear or make up an excuse. I told him exactly what I wanted."

I could practically hear the lightbulb turning on through the coaching call.

And there it was. Sarah had misidentified her Adapted Attachment Stance because she didn't actually understand what the behaviors meant. She thought any need for independence was either Avoidant or Disorganized. When in reality, needing healthy space is a sign of Secure Attachment.

For Sarah, this was a revelation. What she thought was proof that something was wrong with her, was really evidence she was growing.

What looked like Disorganized Attachment on the surface was actually something else. Sarah was navigating Anxious Attachment while trying to set boundaries (*a totally new skill for her!*) And because her nervous system had learned to equate space with abandonment, even healthy separation felt like danger.

STOP THE MUSIC! DID YOU SKIP PART ONE?

Listen, I get it.

You picked up this book, maybe flipped through it, saw Part Two: How to Heal and said, "Perfect! Let's skip the theory and get straight to the good stuff. I just want to fix my relationship problems."

I see you, my impatient friend.

But here's the thing, you can't discover your Attachment Dance without understanding what the dances actually are. And I mean really understanding them. Not just the oversimplified versions you find in Instagram infographics.

If you haven't read Chapters One through Four of this book (Salsa of Uncertainty, Solo Tango, Pendulum Swing Dance, and Smooth Waltz), please *(and I cannot stress this enough)* go back and read them.

Yes, **all of them**. Even the ones that don't initially sound like "you."

Because what I've learned from working with hundreds of clients is that the Attachment Stance you think isn't you? That's often where your biggest blind spots are hiding. The woman who insists she's not Anxious realizes her need to control everything stems from a fear of the unknown. The man who insists he's not Avoidant realizes his "independence" is actually emotional withdrawal.

You need the full picture to discover your real patterns.

"But what about that quiz you mentioned?"

Oh, you want the shortcut? Fine. You can take my Attachment quiz at *danceofattachment.com/quiz*. It's quick and might point you in the right direction.

But *(and this is important, even though my quiz is amazing if I do say so myself)* do not rely on it.

Quizzes are like those "Which Disney Princess Are You?" tests. They're fun and even useful as a starting point, but they can't capture the complexity of how you actually show up in relationships. They can't account for your childhood experiences, your relationship history, or the subtle ways your Attachment patterns have evolved over time.

Your Attachment patterns are too complex, too contextual, and too important to reduce to a quiz score. *(Even if it does come with a snazzy result page.)*

HOW TO DISCOVER YOUR DANCE

If you want to truly discover your Attachment Stance *(not just guess at it)*, you need to do **three** things:

1. Understand each dance deeply *(that's Part One of this book)*.
2. Reflect on your childhood relationships and experiences.
3. Examine your patterns in your last few romantic relationships.

Before we dive in, I want you to grab a notebook, journal, or download your companion workbook at *danceofattachment.com/workbook* so you can fill out the answers as we go along. This isn't passive reading; this is active discovery work.

Step 1: Understand Each Attachment Dance

If you've ever felt confused about why your relationships keep playing out the same way, you're not alone. The first step is understanding what each Attachment Stance really looks like in action.

A lot of people make the same mistake Sarah did. They learn the names and think that is enough. But just knowing the label doesn't change anything. If all you have is a definition, you'll still end up misreading your own behaviors and judging yourself unfairly.

This isn't just about memorizing definitions. You need to understand how each stance shows up in relationships, what triggers it, how it handles conflict, intimacy, and stress, what its core fears and needs are, and how it can be both adaptive and limiting.

Sarah thought she understood Anxious Attachment because she knew she got "clingy." But she didn't understand that her Anxious Attachment can also show up as people-pleasing, over-giving, difficulty setting boundaries, and yes, feeling guilty for having normal human needs like alone time.

She had no idea that Secure Attachment doesn't mean being joined at the hip with your partner. Secure couples can ask for space, enjoy independence, and still be deeply committed to their relationships.

*(Lean in for this part... I'm about to blow your mind... Did you know, Secure couples even have arguments **without** spending three days over analyzing whether they're compatible? Revolutionary stuff, I know!)*

Once Sarah understood what each Attachment Stance actually looked like, we could dig into the real detective work and understand where her patterns originated.

Frequently Asked Coaching Question

"Jenn, what if I relate to all the Attachment Stances?"

Honestly, that makes complete sense. Attachment isn't black and white; it is a spectrum. We all carry pieces of each stance.

You might be Anxious with your partner, Avoidant with your parents, Secure with your best friend, and totally Disorganized when your boss texts "we need to talk." That does not mean you are broken. It means your nervous system is smart. It learned different dances in different rooms.

But here is the part that matters. It is not about picking the perfect label. It is about noticing which pattern drives the bus most often. Conflict, stress, intimacy. That is when your real stance struts onto the dance floor.

The tricky part is that it doesn't feel like a stance when it's happening. It feels like survival, like your body is just doing whatever it must to get through. So instead of obsessing over labels, ask yourself this... When I get triggered, what is my go-to move? Do I chase? Do I shut down? Do I swing back and forth like I can't decide what song I want?

That is the pattern we want to work with. Because once you can name it, you can change it. Once you change it, relationships start to feel a whole lot lighter, safer, and way more fun. And isn't that the whole point? Not to get the label right, but to actually feel better in love. Which means yes, you can finally stop diagnosing yourself with five different stances like it is WebMD for your love life.

Step 2: Reflect on Your Childhood

Your Attachment Stance formed in your earliest relationships. Understanding how your caregivers responded to your needs gives you crucial insight into your current patterns.

Consider your relationship with your parents or primary caregivers. Were they consistently available when you were upset, scared, or hurt? Did they respond to your emotions with comfort and validation, or did they meet you with dismissal and frustration? Think about whether their responses felt predictable, or if their availability depended on their mood, stress level, or other factors. Did you feel safe expressing your needs, or did you learn early on that certain emotions weren't welcome?

Now shift your focus to how your needs were met. When you were hungry, tired, or uncomfortable, were your needs addressed promptly and kindly? When you were excited or happy, were those feelings celebrated and shared, or brushed aside? Think about what happened when you made mistakes, did you receive patience and guidance, or were you met with criticism and punishment? Did you grow up feeling like your needs mattered, or like they were an inconvenience?

Finally, reflect on how you learned to cope with challenges. When things became difficult, did you instinctively seek comfort from your caregivers, or did you learn to handle everything alone? Were you encouraged to express your feelings openly, or did you come to believe that strong emotions were too much for others to handle? And when it came to showing vulnerability, did you feel safe, or did you learn that being "strong" and independent was valued above connection?

Frequently Asked Coaching Question

"But Jenn, I had a decent childhood. This doesn't apply to me."

You might have. Many people with Insecure Attachment patterns had parents who loved them deeply and provided well for them materially. But love and Attachment security aren't the same thing. You can be deeply loved and still develop Nonsecure Attachment patterns if your caregivers were:

- Emotionally unavailable due to anxiety, depression, or their own unhealed Attachment Wounds.

- Physically present but distracted by work, other stressors, or technology.

- Set in their own views about emotions that yours were unintentionally dismissed.

- Dealing with significant life stressors (divorce, financial problems, illness) during your formative years.

This isn't about finding fault. It's about understanding the roots of your current patterns so you can make conscious choices about how you want to show up in relationships now. And let's be real honest, nobody's childhood was perfect. Even the most loving parents miss cues, say the wrong thing, or get overwhelmed sometimes. The point is not to blame, it is to notice. Because once you see where your dance steps came from, you can stop tripping over them and start learning new moves.

Step 3: Examine Your Past Romantic Relationships

The next step is looking at your past relationships. *(I know, I know. You'd rather forget some of them ever happened.)* But this is important because you've likely been replaying the same feelings and behaviors in relationship after relationship, and recognizing those patterns helps you understand what's happening now.

If you always dated people who were hard to pin down and you always felt like you were trying to convince them to choose you *(like Sarah was doing)*, that tells us something important about your patterns. The feelings you're having in your current relationship? They're probably not new; they're echoes of old patterns your nervous system learned long ago.

This means you can't just ignore your past relationships, even the ones you'd rather erase from memory. Those "failed" relationships aren't mistakes; they're data. They show you how your Attachment Stance responds under different conditions, with different types of partners, and in different stages of intimacy.

I know it's tempting to think, "That relationship was a disaster. Let's just pretend it never happened." But here's the thing, research shows that our brains form implicit memories from relationship experiences that continue to influence our behavior even when we're not consciously thinking about those past relationships.[1] Your nervous system remembers everything. The only way to understand your patterns is to look at them honestly, without judgment.

Frequently Asked Coaching Question

"But Jenn, why do I need to look at my past relationships if I've already moved on and I'm over it?"

Because your nervous system hasn't. Even if your mind says, *I'm over it,* your body is still reacting to relationship dynamics based on what it learned before. That old situationship that made you Anxiously Attached, the one where you kept bending over backward just to feel chosen? Your system stored that. Not as logic, but as inner wiring.

And trust me girl, if moving on without looking back actually worked, I would be a millionaire selling that secret in tiny glitter jars. But since no one is buying my imaginary glitter cure, we have to do the real work.

Here is the truth. Looking at your past is not about blame, it is about gathering data. Think of yourself as a detective. Every relationship you have been in leaves behind breadcrumbs that show us what your Attachment Stance expects, fears, and believes it has to do to stay safe. The ex who disappeared when you showed emotion, the partner who only gave you love when you were "low maintenance," the fling who made you feel like too much. They all left imprints.

When we put those pieces together, you start to see the choreography of your own dance. And once you can see the pattern, you can start to choose differently. That is the whole point. Not to rehash the heartbreak, but to learn from it so you do not keep signing up for the same role in the same story with a different actor.

Putting the Steps Together: Sarah's Stance

"I want you to think about your past relationships," I said gently to Sarah. "What patterns do you notice?"

She sighed. "I tend to date guys who are... hard to pin down. Like my ex, Jake. He was charming and fun, but he was always 'figuring things out' about us. I spent two years trying to convince him that committing to me was the right move."

"And how did that feel?"

"Exhausting. I was constantly performing, trying to be the perfect girlfriend. I'd cancel plans with friends if he wanted to hang out, I'd cook his favorite meals, I'd never ask for anything because I didn't want to seem needy."

"What about before Jake?"

"Same thing, different guy. Ryan was emotionally unavailable but in a different way. He'd say he loved me but could never talk about the future. I spent eight months trying to get him to open up."

The pattern was crystal clear, Sarah was drawn to partners who required her to perform for love, just like she'd learned to do in childhood. And when she finally started setting boundaries with Marcus *(like asking for time to read her book)*, she felt guilty because her nervous system interpreted it as failing at her job.

"So with both Jake and Ryan, you never asked for what you needed?" I asked.

"Never. I was too scared they'd think I was too much and leave."

"And with Marcus?"

"I... I actually tell him what I want. Like the reading time thing. I've never done that before."

"How does Marcus respond when you ask for things?"

"He's totally fine with it. He usually just says, 'Okay, enjoy your book' and finds something to do himself." Sarah was quiet for a moment. "Oh my god. The difference isn't that I'm Disorganized with Marcus. The difference is... I'm actually becoming more Secure. After all the work I've done on myself, I'm finally able to ask for what I need without thinking he'll leave me. And I almost missed it because I was so focused on labeling myself as broken!"

Bingo.

WHEN DIY DISCOVERY MAY NOT BE ENOUGH

Sometimes, discovering your Attachment patterns requires more than self-reflection. Sometimes you need a trained professional to help you see what you can't see for yourself.

Consider working with an Attachment-focused therapist, counselor, or coach if you find yourself stuck in the same relationship patterns despite your best efforts to change. Professional support can also help if you have difficulty identifying your emotions or triggers, if your childhood included trauma, neglect, or significant instability, or if you struggle with self-compassion during this discovery process. Most importantly, working with someone trained in Attachment Theory provides the personalized guidance you need for your specific situation.

You can always choose to work with me through my coaching practice, Speak Honest. But more importantly, find someone who truly resonates with you. Someone who understands Attachment Theory deeply and can guide you through this process with compassion and skill. The right support makes all the difference, whether it's with me or another coach who feels like the right fit for you.

The right counselor or coach can see patterns you might miss, help you process difficult emotions that come up during discovery, and provide tools specifically tailored to your Attachment Stance.

Needing help isn't a sign of weakness. It's a sign of wisdom. *(If you think otherwise, that's just your Attachment Wound talking—more on that later.)*

MY OWN DISCOVERY STORY

May 2020.

Fresh out of the most devastating breakup of my life, I sat in my living room with my laptop, ready to solve the mystery of why love felt so damn complicated. I was exhausted from months of replaying every conversation in my head, trying to figure out what I'd done wrong, desperate for some kind of answer.

I typed "Attachment Style quiz" into Google and clicked on the first result. Twenty-three questions later, I was sitting with my new style: **Anxious Attachment with some Secure tendencies**.

Of course, I thought. *That explains everything.* I was the queen of overthinking his texts, analyzing his tone, spiraling when he didn't call back fast enough. Classic Anxious Attachment, right?

If I could go back and talk to that version of myself, I would pat her on the head and say, "Oh, honey, no." (*And then past me would likely swipe my hand away and tell me to fuck off, but I digress...*) Because that's what it feels like when you realize you thought you'd learned the whole dance, but you were only shown half the steps.

Here's what I discovered through my own deep dive into Attachment Theory. My patterns aligned with Disorganized Attachment. That quiz only caught me in one specific moment. When I was raw, heartbroken, and activated by dating someone who was probably dancing the Solo Tango. It was like catching a snapshot in bad lighting, it showed something true but not the whole truth.

Once I started digging into my past relationships, I realized I had acted completely different in my marriage than I did with the man I dated after. In my marriage, I was deeply Avoidant. In the next relationship, I turned into an Anxiously Attached mess. That's when the bigger picture came into focus.

My ex-husband couldn't stand conflict. Not in the conflict-avoidant way, but in the "I can't stop until we're not fighting" way, and it was **exhausting** for me. We couldn't go to bed angry—EVER. Every disagreement had to be talked through immediately, even if I needed space to think. He hated it when I was upset about anything and would try to fix it or make me feel better before I'd even finished processing what I was feeling. And if someone else was bothering me? He'd get more annoyed with them than I was, even though I could handle it myself. Looking back, I can see that he was just being caring and loving. But at the time, it felt like I couldn't breathe without someone hovering over me.

His Anxious Attachment behaviors were triggering my intense Avoidant Attachment responses. The more he pursued connection, the more I retreated. The more he wanted to talk things through, the more I shut down. The more he tried to comfort me when I was upset, the more trapped I felt.

I would literally lock myself in my room. I'd disappear for entire weekends without telling him where I was going. I'd pick fights just to have an excuse to leave the house. I became a master of productive avoidance: suddenly very busy with work, very interested in hobbies, very committed to anything that didn't involve deep conversations.

Looking back at both relationships *(the marriage where I was completely Avoidant and the post-divorce relationship where I was desperately Anxious)* helped me see that I wasn't just one thing. I wasn't just Anxious or just Avoidant, and I DEFINITELY wasn't Secure.

But it wasn't until I looked deeper into my childhood that the full picture emerged. When I started exploring the trauma I'd experienced growing up *(aka the capital-T Trauma I insisted "wasn't that big of a deal" for like... ever)*, everything clicked into place.

That's the power of learning about Attachment Stances, looking at patterns across relationships, AND examining your childhood. One relationship can show you one side of your Attachment Dance. But when you look at the full picture, you see the complete choreography you've been performing all along.

YOUR DISCOVERY HOMEWORK

Now it's your turn to do the real work. Don't rush through this. Discovery is a process, not a one-time event. You can continue reading the next chapters but keep digging. Don't get so bogged down in perfection that you don't progress, but don't also skim so fast that you don't actually spend the time to do the deep work.

Step 1: Understand Each Attachment Stance Deeply

Go back and read Part One of this book if you haven't already. Really understand how each stance shows up, what triggers them, and how they handle relationships. You can't identify patterns you don't know how to recognize.

Step 2: Reflect on Your Childhood

Use the questions from earlier in this chapter to examine your early relationships and experiences. What did love look like in your house? How were your emotions received? What did you learn about getting your needs met?

Step 3: Examine Your Past Relationship Patterns

Look for themes across your last 2-3 serious relationships. What types of partners did you choose? How did you handle conflict and intimacy? What patterns showed up consistently?

Take your time. Be honest. Be curious instead of judgmental. Your patterns made sense given what you experienced. Now you get to choose what comes next.

Discover More with Your Workbook

You'll find three sections that guide you step by step through the process of Discovering your Attachment Stance. I've also added bonus resources like podcasts, links, and even access to free 1:1 support so you don't have to do this work on your own. Take the time to dive in now, because these reflections will set the stage for the next chapter where we begin the next step in your journey: Alleviate your Attachment Wounds.

Scan the QR code or get it at:

danceofattachment.com/workbook

Six

ALLEVIATE YOUR ATTACHMENT WOUNDS

You can't just start dating a Secure man and call it healing. If your wounds are still deep, his steadiness won't feel comforting, it will feel unsettling.

Rachel slumped into our coaching call, looking exhausted.

"Jenn, I know that we figured out that I'm Anxiously Attached, but it doesn't seem to be helping," she announced. "It's like the more I understand my Attachment Style, the more I can't hold onto a relationship. I went through four dates this week! FOUR! And two of them ghosted me after!"

"What about the other two?" I asked.

"Well, one of them is super cute, but he just got out of a relationship, so I'm hopeful. And the other one, there was just no spark there."

"Tell me about the no spark guy..."

"Ugh, Michael? He was... fine. Actually, no, he was great on paper. Texted when he said he would, asked me actual questions about my life, has a stable job, wants a relationship. But sitting across from him at dinner? Nothing. It was like talking to my accountant."

"What did you feel in your body when you were with him?"

"Honestly? Kind of nauseous. He kept looking at me with these earnest eyes, really listening to everything I said, and I just wanted to run. Is that weird? Everyone says I should want a guy who actually pays attention."

"And the guy who just got out of a relationship?"

Her whole energy shifted. "Oh my god, Jake? He's amazing. We had this instant chemistry. We were talking about his ex and how complicated everything is, and I just felt this... pull. Like I could really understand his pain and wanted to be there for him."

"So, the emotionally unavailable guy feels like chemistry, and the emotionally available guy makes you nauseous?"

"When you put it like that..." Rachel paused. "Fuck. That's exactly it, isn't it?"

"Rachel," I said, "what if I told you the reason you can't just 'find a Secure partner' is because there are deeper beliefs running the show? What if your Anxious Attachment is just the visible symptom of invisible wounds?"

"What do you mean?"

"Let's dig deeper. Tell me, what are you most afraid of in relationships?"

She thought for a moment. "That they'll leave. That I'm too much. That once they really get to know me, they'll realize I'm not worth staying for."

"Okay, so what I'm hearing is: I will be abandoned. I am too much. I am not worthy. Would you say those feel true?"

Her eyes filled with tears. "Yes. God, yes. It's like you're reading my diary."

"These are your Attachment Wounds," I explained. "The beliefs underneath your Anxious Attachment. And as long as these wounds are running the show, you'll unconsciously attract partners who confirm them."

"Wait, what?"

"Think about it. If deep down you believe you're unworthy, unlovable, unwanted, and unimportant, what kind of partners will feel familiar to you?"

Rachel's face went pale. "Oh my god. The ones who treat me like I'm unworthy, unlovable, unwanted, and unimportant."

"Exactly. And what happens when someone treats you like you ARE worthy and important?"

"It feels... wrong. Like Michael." Her voice was barely a whisper. "He treated me like I mattered, and it literally made me sick. So what do I do?" she asked. "How do I stop being attracted to the wrong people?"

"We heal the wounds," I said. "We go deeper than your Attachment Stance to the beliefs that created it. We teach your nervous system new truths. And then, only then, will Secure love feel like home instead of work."

This is the piece that most Attachment Theory books miss. You can't just start dating a Secure man and call it healing. If your wounds are still deep, his steadiness won't feel comforting, it will feel unsettling. That's why Rachel felt literally nauseous sitting across from Michael. Her nervous system wasn't wired to recognize safety as love, so it rejected him. Until the wounds are healed, your body will crave what's familiar—**even if what's familiar is chaos.**

Rachel wasn't broken. She wasn't doomed to toxic relationships because there are no "good men out there." She just needed to heal the wounds that were choosing her partners for her.

That's what this chapter is about. Not just understanding your

Adapted Attachment Stance, but healing the wounds that weave through it, dictate it, and keep you stuck in painful patterns, no matter how many books you read or how much you want to change.

WHAT ARE ATTACHMENT WOUNDS, REALLY?

Let's get something straight, ok? Attachment Wounds aren't just "negative thoughts" you can "positive think" away. They're not character flaws or signs you're broken. They're survival adaptations that your nervous system created to protect you.[1]

Think of them as perceptions that solidified into fixed assumptions about yourself, others, and the world. These assumptions helped you survive your early environment, but now they're limiting your potential and sabotaging your relationships.

Here's how they work: Attachment Wounds are limited beliefs about your fundamental worth and safety in relationships. They formed during your childhood through thousands of repeated interactions with your caregivers.[2] Each time your needs weren't met, each time love felt conditional, each time safety felt uncertain, your young developing brain filed away data. *This is how relationships work. This is what I can expect. This is what I'm worth.*

These aren't conscious conclusions you reached. They are implicit knowledge, a wordless bodily knowing that operates faster than thought.[3] They live in your nervous system, not your rational mind, which is why you can think you deserve a healthy relationship while still feeling certain you'll be abandoned.

HOW TO ALLEVIATE YOUR ATTACHMENT WOUNDS

Now that you understand what Attachment Wounds actually are *(those pesky little beliefs that love to sabotage all your relationships)*, the question then becomes, how do we **heal** them?

The approach I teach my clients goes beyond just understanding your wounds. It's about rewiring them at the deepest level. This isn't surface-level work. This is about teaching your nervous system a new truth. I call this practice **Somatic Affirmations**. They're not just words you say in your head. Somatic Affirmations are repeated felt experiences of security in your body. They're about practicing what it feels like to be safe, seen, and secure until your nervous system begins to recognize that as the new normal.

Here's the Process We'll Work Through
First, we identify the specific limited belief that's running your relationships. Not a vague feeling, but the exact wound that gets triggered when things feel unsafe. Then we find its **empowering** opposite. Not just the logical opposite, but the belief that makes your heart flutter with hope.

Next comes the evidence gathering. Your brain has spent years collecting proof that your wound is true. Now we're going to consciously collect evidence for your new empowering belief. Small things at first, like making yourself breakfast, showing up to work, or texting a friend back. These tiny **truths** become the foundation for change.

But here's where it gets different from every self-help approach you've tried. We don't just think these new thoughts; we **feel** them in our bodies. Through **Somatic Experiencing**, we teach your nervous system what "I am enough" actually feels like—the warmth in your chest, the solidness in your belly, the lightness in your shoulders.

This is important, because your body doesn't lie. You can try to repeat affirmations in the mirror all day long, but if your stomach is in knots and your chest is tight, your nervous system isn't on board. Real change comes when your body and your mind are speaking the same language. That's why we slow down, pay attention to sensations, and **anchor** these new beliefs in a felt experience.

Once you've felt this alignment, we start layering it into real life. Maybe you notice yourself pausing before sending that panicked text. Maybe you feel a little more grounded when your partner pulls away instead of spiraling into fear. These micro-moments are signs that the rewiring is taking hold. They prove that your nervous system is learning a new dance. One that feels steady, safe, and secure.

For those ready to go deeper, we practice during alpha-theta brainwave states. That drowsy, receptive state when your brain is most open to rewiring. This is where the real neural pathway changes happen, where we literally carve new routes through that old cornfield of limiting beliefs.

Think of it like laying fresh tracks in the snow. The old paths (the ones of self-doubt and fear) are still there, but the more you ski down the new trail, the smoother and easier it becomes. Eventually, your brain prefers the new path because it feels natural, fluid, and rewarding. That's the magic of practicing in this brain state. You're not forcing change; you're allowing it to take root.

Step 1: Identify Your Attachment Wounds

The first step is to identify your Attachment Wounds. There's a high chance you'll have **many**. (*I had like 15 when I started this process, and I've found more as I've healed.*) But for now, we just want to find the little one holding you back right now.

Start by thinking about your last few relationship triggers. When you felt that panic, that rage, that desperate need for reassurance, what were you afraid was true? What did that situation "prove" about you?

People usually start with beliefs like "I am not enough," "I am unimportant," or "I am excluded." But your wound might be something else entirely. It could be "I am too much," "I am unlovable," or "I am a burden."

For Rachel, after digging deeper into her pattern of being repulsed by available men and attracted to unavailable ones, we tested different wounds. When I said, "I am unimportant," her eyes immediately filled with tears. That's when we knew we'd found it. The belief that had been running every relationship choice she made.

And here's the thing, finding your Attachment Wound often doesn't feel like an "aha!" moment at first. It feels raw. Sometimes it even feels like you've been punched in the gut. That's because these wounds are tender places you've been protecting for years. If you feel a wave of emotional dysregulation *(tearing up unexpectedly, snapping a little quicker than usual, feeling a wave of shame wash over you, or just wanting to pull back and shut down)* you've probably landed on the right wound. That discomfort is your nervous system telling you, "Yes, this is the story I've been carrying."

Frequently Asked Coaching Question

"But Jenn, what if I have ALL the wounds on the list?!"

Girl, it's okay. Breaaaathe. I had them all too. Hell, I started adding new ones to the list as I discovered them. My clients have shared wounds with me that made me go, "Oh shit, that's one too?"

Having multiple wounds doesn't mean you're more broken than everyone else. It means you're human and you've been through some shit. It means your nervous system got creative and tried a bunch of different strategies to keep you safe. That is not weakness, that is survival. And the fact that you are here, asking these questions, means those same strategies didn't kill your ability to heal.

The good news? We're going to tackle them one at a time. Will it take longer to heal multiple wounds? Sure. But you know what? You've been carrying these wounds your whole life. Taking a few months to heal them properly is nothing compared to that.

So pick your starter wound *(the one that keeps hijacking your texts, your trust, and your Tuesday nights)* and let's get to work. Once you see one wound start to shift, the others will not feel as terrifying. Healing has a ripple effect. You do not have to fix every single wound today. You just have to begin.

And let me be clear, this is not about perfection. You will not suddenly wake up as a brand-new person with zero triggers. What actually happens is better. You start catching the patterns faster. You start responding instead of reacting. And that, my friend, is what real freedom feels like.

Step 2: Find the Empowering Belief (The Opposite)

Once you've identified your limiting belief, the next step is to create its positive opposite. This can be surprisingly difficult, not because you don't know the words, but because the belief has been living in you for so long that its opposite might feel unbelievable or out of reach. That's exactly why it matters. Naming the positive opposite begins to open the door to a new possibility.

For example, if your limited belief is "I am excluded," the empowering belief isn't "I am not excluded." Your brain can't work with the absence of something; it needs a positive to move toward. The empowering belief would be "I am included."

But sometimes finding the right opposite requires getting **creative**. If your wound is "I am a burden," what's the opposite? It might be "I am valued," "I am cherished," or "I am a gift." Each of these carries a slightly different energy or a different felt sense in your body.

This is when a **thesaurus** becomes your bestie. Seriously. Look up the opposite of your limited belief and explore different words until one makes you go, "YES, that's what I want to feel." The word that gives you a little flutter of hope? That's your empowering belief.

For Rachel, her "I am unimportant" became "I am important." Simple, direct, and exactly what her nervous system needed to learn. Remember, it does not need to feel 100 percent true yet. It just needs to feel possible, like a crack of light under the door that your nervous system can start moving toward.

Frequently Asked Coaching Question

"Jenn, is [insert word here] an ok empowering belief to use?"

I get this question a lot. So here's my litmus test:

1. Is it positive? Avoid using negatives like "not," "isn't," or "don't." Your brain is much more responsive to solution-oriented beliefs (I am valued) instead of problem-oriented beliefs (I am not a burden)

2. Does it create a positive physical sensation in your body when you say it?

If yes to both, you've got your word.

I've had clients whose first language isn't English use words from their native language because it hits different in their body. THAT'S the power we're looking for. One client's empowering belief was literally "I am a fucking badass" because that's what made her feel powerful—like electricity in her spine. Another used the Portuguese word "querida" (beloved) because "loved" in English felt flat, but "querida" created warmth all through her chest. Just recently a client decided to use the phrase "I am divine." And it has been a game changer for her.

Your word needs to create a somatic response. If "I am valued" feels like nothing, but "I am treasured" makes your whole body soften? That's your word. Trust your body, not your brain, on this one.

Step 3: Find Evidence for Your Empowering Belief

This is the part where talk turns into action. Beliefs do not shift just because you say a pretty affirmation in the mirror. They shift when your nervous system starts to see proof that a new story is possible.

Here's where most people get stuck. Your brain has spent YEARS collecting evidence for your limited belief. Every rejection, every criticism, every moment of loneliness got filed away as proof that your wound was true.

But here's what your brain didn't do, it didn't collect evidence for the empowering belief. It literally filtered out anything that didn't match your existing belief. That's how wounds stay alive, by selective attention.

Now, we're going to manually collect evidence for your empowering belief. And here's the key... **start small**.

You don't need grand gestures or life-changing moments. If your empowering belief is "I am enough," your evidence might be:

- I was enough today because I made myself breakfast.
- I was enough when I showed up to work.
- I was enough when I texted my friend back.
- I was enough when I took a shower.

I know these seem trivial. Your wounded brain will want to dismiss them. "That doesn't count," it'll say. "Anyone can make breakfast."

But that's exactly the point. We're starting where you are, with what you can believe. Because trying to jump from "I'm worthless" to "I'm the most amazing person ever" is like trying to jump across the Grand

Canyon. You need stepping stones.

One or two pieces of **evidence** per day is plenty to start. Quality over quantity. What matters is that you can genuinely acknowledge these moments as true.

When Rachel first tried this, she struggled. "I don't see how I'm important," she said, frustrated. "Nothing big happened today."

"Let's look at your week," I suggested. "Any moments where you felt like you mattered to someone?"

She thought for a minute. "Well... my friends invited me out for drinks next weekend. But that's just—"

"Stop right there. Your friends specifically thought of you and wanted you there. What else?"

"My boss praised my project in front of the whole team yesterday. Said I'd really knocked it out of the park."

"And how did that feel?"

Rachel's eyes got a little misty. "Like... like my work actually mattered. Like I mattered."

"That's your evidence. Your friends want you around. Your boss sees your value. You are important to people in your life."

That's how we start. Not with grand gestures, but with the real moments that prove your wound is misguided. And once your brain has a folder of proof to flip through, your empowering belief starts to stick. It shifts from a whisper of possibility to a voice of truth.

Frequently Asked Coaching Question

"Jenn, do I need to find new evidence every single day?"

Nope! Here's how it works:

In the beginning, find a few solid pieces of evidence and use those same ones for a week straight. Seriously. The goal right now is just building the habit. Your brain needs repetition more than variety.

As you get more comfortable with the practice, you'll naturally start noticing new evidence throughout your week. "Oh, my coworker asked my opinion, that's evidence I'm important."

Eventually *(and this is where it gets magical)*, you'll be finding fresh evidence from THAT VERY DAY. Every night, you'll have new proof of how important, valued, cherished, or loved you are. Once your brain knows what to look for, it spots evidence everywhere. It is like when you buy a red car and suddenly see red cars on every corner. Your evidence has always been there, but now your system is wired to catch it.

But don't rush this progression. Start where you are. Same few pieces of evidence every night for a week? Perfect. That is not cheating, that is rewiring. You are literally re-training your nervous system to trust a new story. And let me tell you, rewiring decades of programming is a way bigger deal than winning some imaginary creativity contest.

Step 4: Feel the Evidence in Your Body

This is where the magic happens. It's not enough to think, "My friends invited me out, so I'm important." You have to FEEL what being important feels like in your body.

Peter Levine, who developed Somatic Experiencing, discovered that trauma and emotional wounds aren't just stored in our minds, they're held in our bodies as incomplete nervous system responses.[4] The only way to truly heal is to complete these responses through felt experience.

So when you identify your evidence like "My boss praised my work," here's what you do:

Close your eyes and bring that moment back. Not just the facts, but the full sensory experience. Where were you standing? What did you see? What did you hear? Now notice, what happened in your body when you received that praise?

Maybe you felt:

- A warmth spreading across your chest.
- Your shoulders dropping and relaxing.
- A lightness in your belly.
- A tingling in your hands.
- Your breath becoming deeper.

Whatever you notice, **stay with it**. Don't judge it or try to change it. Just feel it.

If you're someone who struggles to feel anything in your body *(don't worry, most of us didn't get the "how to feel things" manual either)*, start with temperature and texture. Is this feeling warm or cool? Heavy or light? Moving or still? Sharp or soft?

For Rachel, when she recalled her boss's praise, she noticed a warm, golden feeling in her chest that slowly spread to her shoulders. "It feels like honey," she said, surprised. "Warm and slow and... sweet? Is that weird to say?"

"Not at all," I explained. "That's actually exactly what we're looking for. Your body doesn't speak in abstract concepts like 'importance' or 'worthiness.' It speaks in sensations like temperature, texture, movement, and color. The more specific and unusual your description, the more I know you're truly feeling it in your body rather than thinking about what you should feel."

This is key for everyone doing this work. Your Somatic Experience might feel like honey, or bubbles, or a warm blanket, or tree roots growing down, or a thousand other unexpected sensations. There's no "right" way for importance or enoughness to feel. What matters is that YOU feel it, that your nervous system has a felt reference point for this new truth.

"I am important" now had a **somatic signature** that Rachel could lean into—warm honey spreading from her chest. Her body could remember this feeling and return to it. Not just an idea anymore, but a lived experience.

Spend at least 20-30 seconds with each feeling. Let it develop, spread, and/or change. You're not rushing through a checklist. You're teaching your nervous system a new language. The language of your worth, spoken in sensation rather than words.

Frequently Asked Coaching Question

"I don't feel anything in my body, Jenn. I'm just... numb.
Am I too broken for this?"

Oh, honey, NO. You're not broken. But you know what we just found? Another Attachment Wound! *(See how "I am broken" just snuck in there?)*

Being numb means you learned early that feeling wasn't safe. Your nervous system shut down the feeling department to protect you. That's not broken, that's brilliant survival!

It served and protected you back then, but here's what you can do now. Just write or say your evidence anyway. Don't worry about feeling it yet. Numbness IS a sensation, it's your starting point. Notice it. Where does the numbness live? How thick is it? Does it have a temperature?

Keep writing, "I am resilient" *(if that's the empowering belief for your "I am broken" wound)* every night. Day 2, still numb? Cool, keep going. Day 8? Maybe the numbness feels different. Day 17? Keep writing. Around day 20-something, you might write "I am resilient because I keep showing up for this healing work" and suddenly feel... something. Maybe pride, like a tiny balloon inflating in your chest. Maybe warmth. Maybe just less numb.

That's your nervous system starting to trust that it's safe to feel again. Some people start numb and end up being the ones who feel everything most deeply. You're not behind—you're just starting from a different place.

Step 5: Practice in Alpha-Theta Brainwave State

Want to take this work to the next level? This step is for those ready to create permanent change.

When you think your new empowering belief all day long, eventually it will stick. But practicing it when your brain is in the alpha-theta state? That will make the work go so much **faster**.

It's like hanging your laundry outside. You can hang it up at night and it'll still dry eventually, but it takes a lot longer and doesn't feel as fresh. Hang it up in the morning sun, though, and it dries quickly and easily. Same with rewiring your brain, you want to work with the natural conditions that help it absorb faster.

The alpha-theta brainwave state is when your brain is most ready to absorb your Somatic Affirmations. This is that drowsy, relaxed state right before you fall asleep or just after you wake up. Your conscious mind's defenses are down, and your subconscious is like a sponge, and it is ready to soak up whatever you give it.[5]

If this feels a little hard to wrap your mind around, think about it like this. Imagine standing in a cornfield. The more you walk the same route, the more a trail gets worn down through the stalks. Farmers with big fields create trails so they can get from one place to another. Now imagine your house is on one side and the store you always go to is on the other. There's a path completely worn down from years of walking it. You've taken it thousands of times. That beaten-down trail represents your neural pathway, the one that has been telling you, "I am not enough," "I am unimportant," or whatever your wound happens to be.

It's easy to get from point A to point B because you've laid down the pathway time and time again through every relationship, every rejection, every moment that reinforced this belief. This isn't your fault; it's simply how your brain wired itself early on.

That store you've been going to? It's outdated. It's filled with Twinkies and Diet Coke and all those processed foods from the 90s that we thought were healthy because they were "low fat" (*Spoiler: they weren't*). That store isn't **nourishing** you anymore.

We need a new store. One with fresh fruits, organic vegetables, grass-fed beef, the good stuff that actually feeds your soul. But to get there, you have to create a whole new path through the corn. At first, you can't even see where you're going. The corn is tall, dense, and in your face. Every step is an effort. The old path is right there, clear and easy, calling to you. (*And damn, that Twinkie does sound really good right now!*)

This is exactly what it's like for our brains to create new neural pathways. You want the nourishing, healing, healthy thing. But it's hard to get to, and the old stuff is so familiar, so you cave. You walk that worn path to the old store, grab a Diet Coke, and do the walk of shame back home.

Or in relationship terms, you're in no contact with your ex, you're healing, and then a trailer comes on for the sequel to that movie you both loved. And suddenly your fingers are typing, "OMG, did you see they're making another one!?" Before your brain even catches up, you've hit send.

That's your brain taking the old path. Not because you're weak or stupid. But because that path is still there, still clear, still calling to you when you're tired or triggered or just not thinking.

Frequently Asked Coaching Question

"But Jenn, I've done affirmations for years and nothing changed. Why is this any different?"

Ah, the affirmation burnout. I feel you. Standing in front of the mirror saying, "I am worthy," while your nervous system is screaming, "LIAR!" Yeah, that shit doesn't work.

This is different because regular affirmations are like trying to paint over water damage. Sure, the wall looks better for a minute, but the rot is still there underneath. This practice? We're fixing the actual damage.

First, we're not just saying pretty words. We're backing them with **EVIDENCE**. Your brain can argue with "I am lovable" all day long. It's harder to argue with "My best friend called me crying because she needed MY specific support."

Second, we're **FEELING** it in our bodies, not just thinking it. Your nervous system doesn't speak English. It speaks sensation. When you feel that warmth in your chest as you recall being valued, you're literally teaching your body a new truth.

Third, we're doing it when your brain is actually **RECEPTIVE**. Saying affirmations while you're stressed and rushing to work? Your brain's defensive walls are up. Doing this work in alpha-theta state? It's like the door to your subconscious is wide open.

You're rewiring your neural pathways with evidence, sensation, and repetition. That is the power of Somatic Affirmations.

Putting the Steps Together: Rachel's Wounds

She started with her core wound: "I am unimportant." Her empowering belief became "I am important." Simple, clear, direct.

Every day, she looked for evidence. Her friend texting to check in. Her mom calling to ask her advice about something. Her coworker asking for her input on a project. Small moments that her wounded brain wanted to dismiss, but that proved she mattered to people.

Each piece of evidence, she'd pause and feel it. The warm honey sensation in her chest became her body's **somatic signature** for "I am important." She'd close her eyes for 20-30 seconds and let that feeling spread.

Then every morning, in that drowsy state before properly starting her day, she'd recall yesterday's evidence and feel each one again. Rachel loved doing this with a warm cup of herbal tea for 10-15 minutes, marinating in the truth of her importance. Some days it felt forced. Some days she cried. Some days she felt nothing. Some days she felt everything. Each day, she kept going.

After 30 days, something shifted. When Michael *(remember him? The "boring" available guy?)* texted to ask her out again, she didn't feel nauseous. She felt... curious. Not fireworks, not that chaotic chemistry she was used to, but a gentle warmth.

"It's weird," she told me. "He's the same person, but I'm seeing him differently. Like my body isn't rejecting the idea of being treated well anymore."

That's what this work does. It doesn't magically make you attracted to different people overnight. It slowly, steadily teaches your nervous system that you're worthy of the love you've been rejecting. And once your body truly believes that? Being treated like the queen you are (i.e., having someone see your worth, respect your needs, show up consistently) stops feeling uncomfortable. It stops triggering that urge to run or that voice saying, "This is too good to be true." Instead, being treated well starts to feel... safe. Like coming home.

MY OWN WOUND WORK

Okay, I'm about to tell you something that still makes me cringe, so stay with me here. After the breakup that nearly destroyed me and before I was first learning about the subconscious mind and how to rewire my brain, I was obsessed with my ex. And when I say obsessed, I mean I kept SPREADSHEETS tracking when he would watch my Instagram stories.

Not just the date. We're talking THE. TIME. OF. DAY.

I'd check who viewed my stories constantly *(like every hour, constantly)* just to see if he'd watched. When he did, I'd jot it down in my little spreadsheet of desperation. I felt elated, like I mattered, like he needed to see what I was doing, like I was actually important to him.

When he didn't watch. Devastation. Complete spiral. *What had I done wrong? Was I texting too much? Were my stories boring? Should I post something different?* I'd try new tactics, post thirst traps, anything to bait him into watching.

I'm legit shocked I'm writing this, to be honest. I mean, he could read this! The shame still makes my face hot *(which is a good indicator that I still have work to do on this! Yay healing!)* But girl, here's the thing:

The power in our voice comes from using it. And I want to use mine to let every woman reading this to know that whatever whacked out thing you did after a breakup, you are not the only one. We ALL do dumb shit when our wounds are activated. You're not alone in your spiral girl. I promise.

So there I was, hating myself for keeping this obsessive spreadsheet, as one does. At first, it just felt like evidence that no one was ever going to want me. But then I started learning about what Attachment Wounds are and how they silently choreograph our reactions.

So I thought, what if I didn't shame this part of me? What if I used it as an anchor point for my healing journey? I started observing what was actually happening. When he watched my stories, I felt excitement and warmth, like I was wanted and important. It felt like I was wrapped in a warm blanket, and like my stomach was throwing a dance party. But when he didn't... complete devastation. Like, full-body, burning-hand, chest-tight kind of devastation. Not just being unwanted by him but by the entire world.

Ding ding ding! There they were. My Attachment Wounds. I am unwanted and I am unimportant.

It hit me that those two were really just different sides of the same coin. Whenever I felt unwanted, I also felt unimportant. And whenever I felt unimportant, I was sure I was unwanted. It became a loop that kept feeding itself.

And here's the tricky part, even when good things happened, my brain found a way to discredit them. That's what Attachment Wounds do, they twist the evidence to fit the old story. So, when my mom called to check on me, my mind said, *she has to; she's my mom*.

119

When my friend asked for advice, the voice in my head said, *she was just desperate.* When my son gave me a hug, I dismissed it as, *he just wanted something from me.*

I wanted to quit. Actually, I DID quit for a few weeks because I thought it was bullshit. But then the urge to check if he'd watched my stories came roaring back like an addiction, so I dragged myself back to the practice.

And slowly, something shifted. I started caring less about whether he watched. I started noticing all the ways I WAS important—even to him. The way he'd text me funny memes. How he'd laugh at my jokes. Things I couldn't even let myself feel before because the wound of being unimportant was too heavy to see past. *(More on THAT in the next chapter.)*

My Somatic Affirmation practice evolved over time. At first, I'd write my evidence list every Monday afternoon and use the same evidence all week. After about six months of working on multiple wounds, I started writing fresh evidence each night.

Now? I just collect evidence mentally during the day. At night, I lie in bed and go through each area of my life, telling myself the evidence and feeling it in my body as I drift off to sleep. If I fall asleep before I finish, I just do the rest of the evidence in the morning as I'm waking up. *(Gives me something to do in between hitting snooze 15 times.)*

Your practice will look different from mine, just like it looks different from where I started. It's like going to the gym—my personal trainer's routine looks way more polished than mine ever will. *(I WILL NOT DRINK GREEN JUICE, CHERYL! STOP MAKING ME!)* But I show up and do what I can, and that's all I'm asking of you.

The spreadsheet? Long deleted. The obsession? Gone. The wound? Still there, but quiet now. It whispers sometimes, but it no longer controls my life.

That's what this work does. It doesn't erase your wounds or your embarrassing past. It just makes them... smaller. Less powerful. Until one day, you can write about your most desperate moment in a book and only feel a little bit of shame instead of wanting to die. Progress, not perfection. That's the real transformation, not erasing your wounds but altering your relationship with them.

YOUR ALLEVIATION HOMEWORK

Alright, you ready to do the work?

Great! Because here's the good news, the work of Norman Doidge and other neuroplastic pioneers has shown us that our brains can absolutely change. Even the Attachment patterns that were wired into us as infants.[6]

The key is hitting all the ingredients. We want real evidence *(not just wishful thinking)*, somatic feeling *(not just mental understanding)*, and consistent repetition. Practicing during the alpha-theta brainwave state speeds things up, but even if you only focus on evidence and somatic feeling, you're already doing the work of real rewiring. Without those pieces, affirmations can slip past your nervous system like rain sliding off a windshield.

Somatic Affirmation Practice:

1. **Set aside time before bed or first thing in the morning.** These are the moments when your brain is naturally drifting between conscious thought and deeper states.

2. **Get comfortable, but not so comfortable that you fall asleep.** You want your body at ease, maybe propped up on pillows or sitting in a cozy chair, but still alert enough to stay present.

3. **Take a few deep breaths to relax into that drowsy state.** Notice your shoulders drop, your jaw soften, and your mind start to slow down. This is your entryway into the practice.

4. **Bring to mind your empowering belief.** Choose one that feels true or at least possible, something that challenges the old story you're ready to release.

5. **Recall your evidence from the day.** Think about the small moments that supported this belief. The text you sent, the boundary you held, the laugh you shared.

6. **FEEL each piece of evidence in your body.** Let yourself truly sense it. The warmth in your chest or the buzzing energy in your arms. *(Remember Rachel's honey feeling?)*

7. **Let yourself marinate in these feelings for 10–15 minutes.** That's all it takes. No forcing, no striving, just soaking in the truth that you are safe, capable, and worthy. In time, this becomes less of an exercise and more of a way of being.

Every time you do this in the alpha-theta brainwave state, you're pushing down more corn stalks, making that new path clearer. The old path to the Twinkie store? It becomes less and less defined. And one day, you'll realize the new path *(the one leading to real healthy nourishment)* has become automatic.

Do this for 30 days minimum. Why 30? Because research shows it takes 21-66 days to form new neural pathways,[7] and I've found 30 is the sweet spot to start. It's long enough to see real change but not so long that you'll get overwhelmed and quit on day 5.

Here's the truth: your brain doesn't hit day 21 and go, "DING! New habit installed!" Brains are way more complex than that. Some people feel a shift at 21 days; others need the full 66 or even longer. After your first 30 days, check in with yourself. How are your reactions changing? Do you need another 30 days to really solidify this new path? Trust what you feel.

You're not just thinking happy thoughts, you're literally rewiring your brain's fundamental patterns. And just like building muscle at the gym, some people need more reps than others.

The important part of the Somatic Affirmation practice is finding what works for you. Maybe you're a voice memo person. Maybe you need the ritual of writing. Maybe you like to do it in the morning when you're brushing your teeth.

Some people record themselves reading their evidence and play it during this drowsy state. Rachel liked to hold a warm cup of herbal tea and let the physical warmth remind her of her honey feeling. There's no wrong way, just your way.

When I first started this type of healing work, I wrote everything out and read it before bed every night. Having it on paper made it real and harder for my wounded brain to dismiss. *(You can find journal prompts specifically designed for this practice in the companion workbook.)* Now, after years of doing this, I just run through my evidence as I'm lying in bed, feeling each piece in my body before I drift off.

Even as you move on to the next steps in our D.A.N.C.E. practice, remember this isn't a one-time thing. It's a forever journey, and I want this to become your new normal. Think of it like those physical health recommendations we always hear. Drink 64oz of water, aim for 10k steps, go to the gym 3 times a week.

Most of us don't hit them perfectly every day, but knowing what's good for us helps us keep moving in the right direction. It's the same here. But this is for your mental fitness. Of course, you'll miss days when life gets busy or you're too tired, but the point is to keep making it a consistent effort.

That's what rewires your brain. And when I say, "new normal," I don't mean pressure or perfection. I mean a supportive rhythm that helps you feel steady and secure.

Because here's what I know: 10-15 minutes a day is all it takes to stop being attracted to people who can't love you right. 10-15 minutes to teach your nervous system you're worthy of the good ones. 10-15 minutes to finally stop choosing partners based on wounds that were never your fault. 10–15 minutes to stop doing the dumb shit that is holding you back from the relationships you deserve.

That's less time than you spend scrolling Instagram. Less time than you spent analyzing his last text. Less time than you wasted wondering why you weren't enough. Less time than keeping a spreadsheet documenting all the times he watched your stories. *(Wait... is that one just me?)*

You ARE enough. You always were. Your nervous system just needs to learn it too. 30 days. 10-15 minutes. Your whole love life is waiting on the other side.

Alleviate and Track It in Your Workbook

If you're the type who likes to have all your shit organized in one place *(hi, sames),* open your workbook. For this chapter, it's got all the Somatic Affirmation exercises laid, plus a 30-Day Tracking Chart to help keep you consistent. So you can actually DO this work instead of just reading about it and thinking "that sounds nice" while you continue to go out with emotionally unavailable men named Brad.

Scan the QR code or get it at:
danceofattachment.com/workbook

Seven

NURTURE YOUR ATTACHMENT NEEDS

The problem isn't that you have needs. It's that you were taught to treat them like character flaws.

"I'm so sorry to bother you with this, but..."

Lauren read her draft text aloud during our coaching call, her voice shrinking with each word. I watched her shoulders curl inward as she shared the message she wanted to send her boyfriend, Zack. It was a simple request to spend more time together, but she'd already apologized three times in one paragraph.

Sorry for bothering you. Sorry if this is too much. Sorry if I'm being needy.

"I deleted it and started over," she continued, looking down at her phone, "but listen to the rewrite, 'Hey babe, I know you're super busy with work and I totally understand, but I was wondering if we could hang out this weekend? Only if you want to, no pressure. But if you can't, that's totally fine too.'"

I could practically see her cringing through the screen. "How does it feel to read that back?" I asked.

"Exhausting," Lauren admitted, finally looking up at the camera. "It's like I'm begging for permission to want time with my own boyfriend."

Lauren had been my client for three weeks, and this pattern showed up in every session. She craved connection, closeness, and quality time but packaged every need in layers of apologies, disclaimers, and escape routes. She'd learned early that having needs made her "high maintenance." That asking for things made her "demanding." That expressing what she wanted made her "too much."

So she'd mastered the art of asking for nothing while desperately hoping someone would magically give her everything.

"Tell me about Zack," I said. "How does he usually respond when you do express your needs?"

"That's the thing... he's amazing." Lauren's face softened slightly. "He loves me, shows up consistently, genuinely wants to make me happy. He's never made me feel bad about needing things. But every time I approach him with a need, it feels like I'm begging for scraps instead of asking for what I deserve."

"So the guilt isn't coming from him?"

"No," Lauren said quietly, fidgeting with her coffee mug. "It's all me. I just don't understand why I feel so guilty about wanting time with my own boyfriend. This is all in my head."

"Let's go deeper," I suggested, leaning forward on my own screen. "What happened when you expressed needs as a kid?"

Lauren's posture changed, her voice becoming softer. "Oh, my mom... she tried her best. But she was overwhelmed. Single mom, working two jobs, dealing with my little brother who had special needs. Whenever I needed something—help with homework, a ride somewhere, even just to talk—I could see how tired she looked."

"So what did you learn to do?"

"I learned to need less," she said. "To be the easy kid. To handle things myself. To not add to her plate."

"And now you're applying that same strategy with Zack?"

Lauren was quiet for a moment, staring off-camera. "Oh my God. Yes. I apologize for taking up space in my own relationship. I feel guilty for wanting my boyfriend to prioritize me. I act like my needs are burdens instead of... what are they supposed to be?"

"Invitations," I said. "Your needs are invitations for deeper connection."

"That sounds nice, Jenn," Lauren said with a laugh that wasn't quite happy. "But it doesn't feel true."

What Lauren couldn't see yet was that her chronic apologizing wasn't politeness. It was a symptom. A symptom of her Attachment Needs that had been dismissed, minimized, and pushed underground for so long that she'd forgotten they were valid.

She wasn't "needy." She was normal. She wasn't "too much." She was human.

And she was about to learn the difference between having needs and being needy. A difference that would transform not just how she communicated, but how she saw herself.

WHAT ARE ATTACHMENT NEEDS & WHY THEY MATTER

The problem isn't that you have needs. It's that you were taught to treat them like character flaws.

So when you really want your boyfriend to buy you flowers, you tell yourself you're being "needy." When you crave quality time together, you worry you're being "clingy." When you need reassurance after a fight, you convince yourself you're being "too much."

But what if I told you that wanting flowers isn't needy. Flowers just means you value beauty, thoughtfulness, and emotional connection. Craving quality time means closeness and consistency matter to you. Needing reassurance means emotional safety is important to you. These aren't flaws, they're signals. These are the ways your nervous system says, *this is what fills me up.*

Think of it like this: there's a great little book called *How Full Is Your Bucket?* by Tom Rath and Donald O. Clifton. It's a quick read built around a simple but powerful idea that every person walks around with an invisible bucket. And every interaction we have with others either fills that bucket or drains it. A kind word adds water. Whereas a harsh comment tips some out.

When I first came across this book, the image stuck with me. It gave me language for something I'd felt my whole life, the sense that people could pour into me or drain me with even the smallest actions. But as helpful as the picture was, I always thought something was missing. Because in my relationships, my partners would show me they were pouring into me, and yet I couldn't feel it.

While the bucket metaphor is powerful, it's also incomplete. What it doesn't explain is why some of us can't seem to receive the love given to us, no matter how much gets poured in. Imagine how that must feel for the other person. To be kind, to love, to give, and then to be told it's not enough. Oof, right?

So, what's really keeping us from feeling the connection, love, and safety we long for? It might not be that our partners aren't pouring into our buckets. It might be that our Attachment Wounds have poked holes in our invisible needs buckets, and everything just keeps leaking out.

Each hole has a story. One forms when you asked for comfort and your mom told you to stop being a drama queen. Another when you needed attention, but your dad was too busy to notice. Another when you reached out for love from your family and were met with silence or shame. Over time, those painful punctures add up. So even when someone is pouring into you, it leaks right back out. You finally get exactly what you wanted and still end up feeling empty.

Which raises the question: *What are we supposed to put in our buckets in the first place?* The answer is your Attachment Needs. Your Attachment Needs are made up of both Macro and Micro Needs. At the top are your **Macro Needs,** which are the six big human needs identified by Tony Robbins. Those needs are Connection, Growth, Significance, Certainty, Variety, and Contribution.[1] And every single human being needs them in order to feel fulfilled.

But underneath these Macro Needs are your **Micro Needs**, the tiny, daily, real time requirements that pop up throughout your day. For example, under your Macro Need of **Connection**, you might have Micro Needs for acceptance, family, touch, and trust. Whereas under your Macro Need of **Significance**, you might want recognition, achievement, or validation. And under **Certainty**, you might crave routine, financial security, comfort, or predictability.

Your Micro Needs are like your emotional fingerprint. They are unique to you and only you. Learning what your Attachment Needs are is exactly what we're here to figure out.

The reason this is so important is because research from the Gottman Institute shows that couples are seven times more likely to be satisfied in their romantic relationships when they understand both their own needs and their partner's needs.[2] **Seven times!** That tells us that we aren't supposed to be less needy, we actually need to learn our needs.

The problem is, when you don't know what your needs are, you end up using strategies that don't work, or worse, strategies that quietly sabotage everything you've worked toward.

Your subconscious is constantly trying to meet your Attachment Needs, whether you're aware of it or not. Every behavior is a strategy. Even reading this book is a strategy. Maybe you're here for personal growth, seeking validation for how you've been feeling, or maybe you just thought the cover looked pretty. *(Which, by the way, still counts! That's a totally valid need for beauty, inspiration, and the quiet hope that maybe this time, something will finally click.)*

Once you finally learn to identify your needs, meet them yourself, and receive what is being poured into your bucket, relationships will stop feeling so damn hard. Your bucket begins to actually hold your needs, and what's poured in finally has space to stay and sustain you.

HOW TO NURTURE YOUR ATTACHMENT NEEDS

Now that you understand what Attachment Needs are, let's talk about how to nurture them. This isn't about eliminating your needs or becoming completely self-sufficient. It's about creating a sustainable system where you're not desperately outsourcing your worth to other people while also not trying to meet every need on your own.

And that is the power of identifying your needs, meeting them with care, and learning to receive without guilt. When you stop seeing your needs as flaws and start honoring them as truth, everything shifts. Your **bucket** begins to fill and stay filled. Your nervous system starts to settle. And your rhythm *(the one that's been thrown off by years of over-giving, guessing, and ghosting yourself)* finally begins to reset.

Ready to reset your rhythm?

Step 1: Identify Your Attachment Needs

Identifying your Attachment Needs begins with radical honesty about yourself. This isn't about who you **think** you should be. It's about who you **actually** are right now.

I want you to answer these questions with complete honesty. Please do us both a favor and skip the idealized version of yourself and focus on reality. Instead of saying, "I invest my money wisely and spend my free time volunteering," tell the truth, "I spend my money on skincare products and my free time binge-watching reality TV."

Ask yourself these revealing questions:

- What do I spend my money on?
- How do I spend my free time?
- Who do I genuinely enjoy hanging out with?
- What TV shows do I watch or books do I read?
- Who am I following on social media and why?

Now here's the fun part... connecting the dots. Look back at all your answers. What needs are hiding behind your habits? If you spend your money on travel, maybe you're craving adventure. If your free time is filled with book clubs, maybe you're seeking connection and shared experiences. Even the people you follow online can tell you so much about the needs that matter most to you.

If you're hosting game nights, you're probably craving connection, playfulness, and maybe a little friendly competition. If you're deep in a fantasy book under a blanket, then adventure, comfort, creativity, and imagination might be high on your list.

Not sure what needs your habits are pointing to? Here's a short list of some common Micro Needs to help you start decoding your patterns. I want you to find your top 10 needs, and hold onto them for later:

- **Connection:** emotional connection, touch, quality time, verbal affirmation, belonging, acceptance, compassion, trust, inclusion, family, understanding.

- **Significance:** recognition, achievement, approval, status, uniqueness, validation, respect, influence, purpose, beauty, authenticity, admiration

- **Certainty:** routine, financial security, predictability, safety, structure, control, reliability, consistency, stability, support.

- **Variety:** adventure, autonomy, creativity, discovery, excitement, exploration, freedom, playfulness, spontaneity, novelty, flexibility, joy, inspiration, variety, fun.

- **Growth:** learning, personal development, challenge, skill-building, self-improvement, progress, wisdom, expansion.

- **Contribution:** helping, impact, community, giving, service, teaching, mentoring, supporting, equality, generosity.

Frequently Asked Coaching Question

"But Jenn, I have EVERY NEED!! See, I AM needy!"
Cries into Cheez-It box

First of all, pass the Cheez-Its. Second of all, you're not too much… you're just finally being honest with yourself.

Of course it feels like you have every need when you've spent years suppressing, ignoring, or shaming them. When your needs haven't been met consistently, your nervous system goes into high alert. It becomes hyper-attuned to anything that might get you even a drop of what you've been craving. That doesn't mean you're broken. It means you're brilliant at surviving.

Having a lot of needs doesn't make you needy. It makes you aware. The goal isn't to eliminate your needs. It's to get curious about which ones feel the loudest right now and why. From there, we can figure out which ones are most important to meet right now *(hello, self-soothing and solo dance parties)* and which ones might require a bit more connection and communication.

Step 2: Meet Your Own Needs First (The 50% Rule)

Here's where you learn to fill up your buckets half way, all on your own. This is the foundation that changes everything about how you show up in your relationships.

Remember, the goal has never been to fill your buckets completely on your own. We're not meant to meet every need solo. But it's also not healthy to leave them completely empty, desperately waiting for someone else to fill them. I'm only asking for 50%.

Think of it this way, there's a world of difference between asking for a glass of water because you're kinda thirsty versus asking because you think you'll die of dehydration without it. One comes from strength and choice. The other comes from desperation and fear.

This isn't about independence, it's about empowerment. When you can meet half your needs yourself, you stop outsourcing your emotional survival to other people. You approach relationships from abundance instead of lack. When your buckets are already halfway full, you can ask for what you need without the crushing weight of thinking, *if they don't give me this, I'll be devestated*. That shift, from desperate to empowered, transforms every interaction.

For each of your top needs, brainstorm simple, accessible ways to meet it yourself. Need beauty? Buy yourself flowers, create a beautiful workspace, or take a walk somewhere visually stunning. Need playfulness? Watch a comedy special, play with a pet, or try a new hobby that makes you laugh. Need emotional connection? Journal about your feelings, have a meaningful phone call with a friend, or practice self-compassion. Need adventure? Explore a new neighborhood, try a cuisine you've never had, or take a different route to work.

This practice creates a fundamental shift in your relationship dynamics. Instead of showing up empty-handed, hoping someone else will pour into you, you arrive already partially resourced. You can give from overflow rather than deficit. You can receive without guilt because you're not completely dependent. When your needs become invitations for deeper connection rather than desperate pleas for survival. That's when everything changes.

Frequently Asked Coaching Question

"But Jenn, isn't my partner supposed to meet my needs?
Doesn't he want to make me happy?"

Great question! Your partner absolutely wants to make you happy. But when you're operating from an empty bucket, even his best efforts feel like not enough.

Look at it this way, if you're thirsty and ask someone for water but they say no, how will you feel? You'll probably be okay, because you had some water earlier and know you can get more water later. You're partly filled up, and you have a plan just in case.

Now imagine you haven't had water in 5 days. You're dehydrated, desperate, you have no idea where you can find water, and you beg the first person you see for water. And in that moment they say, "No I can't give you any water." How do you think you'll feel?

Devastated. Scared. Distraught. You might think you're going to die. And this is literally what your body thinks when you ask your boyfriend for a hug after work and he says, "Hold on, babe, let me put my stuff down first." REJECTION! The worst. And your body reacts with so much pain you'd think you were also dying of dehydration.

It's why Lauren couldn't say, "Hey, wanna hang out Saturday?" What if he said no? DEVASTATION. Because he was her only source of so many needs. She relied on him to meet them instead of having them half way filled and having a plan in case he said no.

Step 3: Learning to Actually Receive Your Needs

We need to talk about the biggest issue with needs, which is that we can't actually receive them.

Your partner buys you flowers? You ask what he did wrong. He plans a hiking date? You're mad it's not the restaurant you hinted at. He surprises you with a weekend getaway? You stress about whether you look good enough or if you're being too much trouble.

Girl, we do this to ourselves and it HAS to stop.

These are the holes in our invisible buckets we talked about earlier. You can fill your bucket halfway, but if you have holes from all these Attachment Wounds ("I am not enough," "I am unlovable," "I am a burden"), then even when we pour into ourselves, it leaks right out.

So when you finally ask your husband to plan a date night, you can't even enjoy it because your brain is spiraling: *Am I being a burden? Did I do enough to deserve this?* Meanwhile, he's just Googling which wine pairs best with the sirloin.

This is where the work from the previous chapter becomes crucial. As we heal our Attachment Wounds, the holes in our buckets begin to close. We can ask for what we need and actually receive it.

If you ask to spend Sunday together and he suggests watching the game with friends, you can appreciate that he wants to include you while also saying, "I was hoping for some one-on-one time today." But it won't come from a place of lack *(remember the water analogy?)*. Instead, it comes from abundant empowerment.

Frequently Asked Coaching Question

"But Jenn, I start to feel guilty when other people meet my needs, is this normal?"

OMG, that is a resounding yes. It's more common than you think.

If no one ever taught you that your needs were allowed, valid, and safe, then of course you're going to feel guilty when someone tries to meet them.

That guilt you feel? It's not proof that your need was too much. It's proof that the caregiver who was supposed to attune to your needs couldn't. Maybe because they were overwhelmed, unavailable, emotionally immature, or dealing with their own trauma.

As a child, you didn't have the ability to step back and think, *Maybe my parent is overwhelmed, wounded, or unavailable.* That kind of perspective comes with a fully developed brain, and you didn't have that yet. So instead, like all kids do, you turned the pain inward. You made it about you. *I must be the problem. I must be too much. Too sensitive. Too needy. Too emotional.*

The reality is it never actually made sense. It just felt safer to believe you were the issue than to face the terrifying possibility that the people responsible for your care couldn't meet your needs.

Now, as an adult, that guilt is just the echo of a story you were never meant to carry. But the good news is you don't have to carry it anymore.

Putting the Steps Together: Lauren's Needs

Six months into our work together, Lauren emailed me a screenshot that made me smile.

Lauren to Zack: "Hey babe, I've had a really stressful week and could really go for some of those support snuggles. Wanna do something together tonight?"

Zack: "Of course! Some coworkers are going out after work tonight, you wanna come?"

Lauren: "That's sweet of you to include me! I was actually hoping for some one-on-one time where we can catch up. Could we do dinner at home instead?"

Zack: "Absolutely. I'll grab ingredients on my way home."

The Lauren from our first session would never have clarified what she needed. She would have either said yes to the group hangout and felt resentful the whole time, or gotten hurt that he "didn't understand" what she was asking for and shut down completely.

But this Lauren had done the work. She'd identified that two of her core needs were **emotional connection** and **quality time**. She'd learned to meet those needs herself through journaling, calling friends for heart-to-heart conversations, and taking herself on solo coffee dates where she could process her thoughts.

Most importantly, she'd plugged the holes in her bucket that whispered, "Asking for what you need makes you a burden" and "If he really loved you, he'd just know."

"Six months ago, I would have been crushed that he suggested the group thing," she told me later. "I would have thought he didn't want alone time with me. But instead, I could see he was trying to solve my problem. He just needed more information about what I actually wanted."

That's what's possible when you stop treating your needs like they're inconveniences and start treating them like the roadmap to deeper connection they really are.

MY OWN NURTURING STORY

I used to be the queen of unmet needs and didn't even know it.

For years, I thought I was just "low maintenance." I prided myself on not needing much, on being the cool wife who never asked for anything. But what I was actually doing was starving myself emotionally while pretending I wasn't hungry.

Our ten-year anniversary was the moment everything became crystal clear. I had been so excited for this milestone. I kept dropping hints about wanting to celebrate, expecting him to plan something special. Yet, when he asked me what I wanted to do for our anniversary, I said I wasn't bothered. *(Narrator's voice: She was, in fact, very bothered.)*

When it became obvious he hadn't planned anything, I scrambled to organize a trivia night and drinks at our favorite bar. Even that felt like a win to me. At least we were celebrating, right? But the whole night, he barely talked to me. He was present physically, but emotionally? He felt a million miles away. I sat across from him, feeling more alone than if I'd stayed home by myself.

I was devastated. This was our ten-year anniversary, and I felt like I was celebrating with a stranger who was simply doing me a favor by even showing up.

Looking back now, I can see that's just his personality. He's not naturally celebratory or emotionally expressive. In fairness, after ten years, we were already in a pretty bad rut. We'd go on to separate about six months after that anniversary. But at the time, all I knew was that I needed more from him and had absolutely no idea how to ask for it.

I needed him to be excited about our milestone. I needed him to express appreciation for our marriage. I needed him to connect with me emotionally, to make me feel like this anniversary mattered to him too. But instead of saying any of that, I sat there silently fuming and expected him to read my mind and magically transform into the emotionally available partner I was craving.

When he didn't, I felt rejected and unloved. I started that very familiar spiral of "If he really loved me, he would just know" and "I shouldn't have to ask for basic consideration." I made his personality about my **worth** and his communication style about my **value**.

It was the start of realizing I needed more but not knowing how to communicate that. I had spent a decade expecting mind-reading instead of using my words. I had confused his introversion with rejection, his different love language with lack of love.

That anniversary was a turning point because it showed me how I so desperately needed to learn the language of my own needs. I couldn't keep expecting people to be mind readers while refusing to tell them what was actually in my mind.

Years later, with a different partner and a whole new understanding of myself, I finally got to practice what I'd never known how to do before.

For our third anniversary, I communicated to my current husband just how important it was to me that we do something special, and that I felt a little disappointed that nothing had been planned yet. I didn't micromanage. I didn't spiral. I communicated with confidence *(more on that in the next chapter)*, and I honored my needs because this time, I trusted the foundation we'd built. I knew he loved me. I knew I loved him. I knew we'd be fine even if nothing happened, and I trusted he'd listen and understand for next year.

THAT'S the power of **knowing** your needs.

And guess what? He pulled off an amazing anniversary. He booked a stay at the hotel where we got married, stocked it with all my favorite snacks, and totally spoiled me with sweet, thoughtful gifts. And for the first time, I felt **truly fulfilled** in a relationship on an anniversary.

What changed? I approached it from abundance, not desperation. I came from a place of "this matters to me" instead of "if you don't do this, you don't love me." I could receive what he gave me because my bucket didn't have holes in it anymore.

The woman who used to pride herself on needing nothing learned that real pride comes from knowing exactly what you need and having the courage to ask for it.

YOUR NUTURE HOMEWORK

Ready to stop operating from empty buckets? This work isn't really complicated, but it does require honesty. You're going to identify what you actually need, learn to meet those needs halfway, and start plugging the holes that keep you from receiving them.

Step 1: Identify Your Needs

First, you're going to sit down and take a good, honest look at your actions, choices, and behaviors using a few simple questions. And I do mean **honest**. If you spend money on emotional-support water bottles instead of a financial advisor, or if you binge steamy novels instead of reading *The Body Keeps the Score*, that's not a failure—that's data. We're not judging your coping strategies here. We're just trying to understand what they're actually doing for you.

Start by asking yourself some honest questions: What do you do without even thinking? What actually brings you joy? What can't you live without? What do you **wish** you were doing more of? What patterns show up in how you think, how you spend your time, and where your money goes?

Once you've reflected, pull up the Micro Needs list and see what jumps out now that you're seeing the patterns more clearly. Highlight the ones that feel true **right now**. Then pick your top 10 and write them down somewhere you'll actually see them, not just in a journal you never open again.

Step 2: Fill Your Buckets Halfway

Now that you've identified your top needs, it's time to start filling your own bucket... at least halfway.

Think of it like this, your needs bucket has to be filled regularly, or you'll end up feeling drained, disconnected, and reactive. And while yes, other people **can** pour into your bucket, it's your job to pour into yourself at least 50% of the way. That's what this step is all about.

For each of your top 10 needs, brainstorm one or two simple, doable ways you can begin meeting them on your own. This isn't about being self-sufficient to a fault; it's about gently filling your own bucket ways that make feel fulfilled. Not because you must do it all alone, but because you deserve to experience what it feels like to meet your needs without shame or apology.

Think small and soft. If your need is **comfort**, maybe that looks like rewatching your favorite feel-good TV show in your coziest blanket. If your need is **emotional connection**, it might be writing in a journal and letting yourself feel seen by yourself. If you're craving **touch**, maybe it's a hot bath, lotion on your skin, or cuddling up with a pet. These aren't luxuries, they're little love notes to your nervous system.

Step 3: Repairing the Holes in Your Bucket

Now that you've identified your top 10 Attachment Needs and you're learning how to meet them halfway, it's time to explore what's getting in the way of **receiving** them. Because even when someone tries to pour into your bucket, if there are old wounds poking holes in the bottom, that effort will leak right out.

Under each of your top 10 needs, take a moment to name the belief or fear that's been leaking out of it. This is the story your nervous system picked up along the way. If your need is **recognition**, but you carry a wound that whispers, "I am undeserving," write that down. If your need is **emotional connection**, but you've internalized, "I am too much," note it. These beliefs aren't the truth. They are just the protective stories you've learned to carry.

Remember, you're not just learning something new; you're unlearning decades of programming. That takes time. Sometimes years. So take it one day at a time.

In addition to your Attachment Needs homework, be sure to continue your Somatic Affirmation practice from the previous chapter. Fifteen minutes a day is how you plug the holes in your buckets and teach your nervous system that it's safe to receive.

Alleviate. Nurture. Repeat. That's how the healing sticks.

Needs Pair Best with the Workbook

Kind of like wine and cheese. Or texting and regret. Whether you've already downloaded it and you're opening it up with us now, or you still need to go grab it *(don't worry, I won't tell anyone)*, just know the workbook is your go-to for diving deeper. Inside you'll find the full needs assessment, micro needs list, and journal prompts to help you make this stick.

Scan the QR code or get it at:
danceofattachment.com/workbook

Eight

COMMUNICATE WITH CONFIDENCE

The more specific you can get about your emotions,
the clearer your communication will be.

"It's all ruined! I fucked it all up!"

Maya's voice was shaking during our coaching call the day after what she described as "the fight to end all fights" with her boyfriend, Alex. Her eyes were still puffy, and I could tell she'd been replaying the whole thing all night.

"I completely lost it, Jenn," she said, her voice full of shame. "Alex came home late from work again without texting, and instead of just saying I missed him or asking about his day, I went straight into attack mode. I yelled at him that he never communicates, and he doesn't even care about me. It was like I became someone else." Her head dropped, eyes fixed on the floor.

"Oh, Hun, that sounds rough. Tell me more, what happened next?" I asked gently.

"He got defensive, obviously. Started listing all the times he DOES communicate and how unfair I was being. Then I started crying and told him he was gaslighting me. It was a complete mess. We both ended up sleeping in separate rooms, and this morning things were so awkward we could barely look at each other."

Maya had been working with me for a few months. And she had made huge progress by identifying her needs and doing or Somatic Affirmations. The more Maya learned about her needs and started believing she deserved to have them met, the more she wanted to speak up for herself. The problem was, it kept coming out all jumbled. Like emotional word-vomit instead of clear communication.

"The thing is," she continued, looking frustrated and defeated, "I know what I actually wanted to say. I wanted to tell him I'd been look-ing forward to seeing him all day. I wanted to ask if everything was okay at work. I wanted to feel close to him, not fight with him. But sometimes I wonder if I was better off before all this healing work, you know? At least then, I just stayed quiet and avoided conflict. Now I know I deserve more, but asking for it seems to make it worse."

"So what happened between wanting connection and starting a fight?" I asked.

"It's like my mouth took over before my brain could catch up. I felt that familiar anxiety spike when he walked in the door looking stressed, and suddenly, I was in full attack mode. All that work we've been doing just... disappeared."

What Maya didn't realize was that she was missing a crucial piece of the Attachment healing puzzle. Yes, she had learned to identify her Attachment Needs and she was working on healing her Attachment Wounds, but she hadn't learned how to confidently communicate when her nervous system was activated.

That's where most women get stuck. They start healing, they learn their needs, and they begin to see they deserve more. So, they jump at the first chance to blurt out all their new ideas. But I want you to slow down. It takes time for your nervous system to catch up to your new beliefs.

And, if you're not careful, you can undo so much of your progress by slipping into the belief that you "messed up" or "failed" at communi-cating. The truth is, Maya wasn't broken, and neither are you. She just needed to learn how to do these three thing: **Regulate, Validate, and Collaborate**.

WHAT IS CONFIDENT COMMUNICATION, REALLY?

Let's get something straight, confident communication isn't about never feeling nervous, never getting triggered, or having the perfect words in every situation. It's not about becoming a Zen Master who floats above human emotions.

Confident communication is about having tools to work **with** your nervous system instead of being hijacked by it. It's about creating space between stimulus and response so you can choose how you want to show up, even when you're feeling activated.

Research by Dr. John Gottman shows us exactly why this matters. His famous *Four Horsemen* study found that criticism, contempt, defensiveness, and stonewalling are the strongest predictors of relationship failure.[1] Here's the hopeful part, these destructive patterns aren't personality flaws. They're responses that happen when our nervous systems are dysregulated.

Think about Maya's situation. She wasn't necessarily wrong to feel upset when Alex came home late and distracted. That's very normal human connection-seeking behavior. The problem wasn't how she was feeling. It was that she didn't have a system for processing those feelings before they turned into accusations.

Here's what confident communication actually looks like:

- **Feeling** your emotions without being controlled by them.
- **Expressing** your needs without apologizing for having them.
- **Listening** to understand, not just to respond.
- **Collaborating** on solutions instead of assigning blame.
- **Repairing** when conversations go sideways.

This isn't about becoming a perfect communicator. It's about becoming a conscious one. Someone who can stay present and connected even when things get messy.

HOW TO COMMUNICATE WITH CONFIDENCE

After years of studying Attachment Theory, relationship research, and working with hundreds of clients, I've developed a simple but powerful framework for communication that honors both your emotional reality and your relationship goals.

It's called **Regulate, Validate, Collaborate,** and it will change how you navigate every difficult conversation for the rest of your life.

Step 1: Regulate (Using the R.A.I.S.E. Method)
Before you can communicate effectively, you need to get your nervous system on board. When you're in fight-or-flight mode, your prefrontal cortex *(aka the part of your brain that does the adulting)* goes offline.[2] You literally cannot access your best thinking or clearest communication when you're dysregulated.

Regulation is the difference between reacting and responding. Reacting is snapping back, shutting down, or saying something you regret because your body feels threatened. Responding is pausing long enough to steady yourself so you can choose words that are aligned with who you want to be. When you regulate, you create that crucial pause, the space that lets you respond with intention instead of react from fear.

That's why regulation comes first. Always.

Here's the **R.A.I.S.E.** method I teach all my clients:

*R*emove yourself from the triggering situation, even briefly. This might mean saying, "I need a five-minute break to collect my thoughts" or literally stepping into another room. You're not avoiding the conversation; you're preparing for it.

*A*nchor yourself in your body using grounding techniques. Feel your feet on the floor. Take three deep breaths. Notice five things you can see around you. The goal is to shift from emotional overwhelm back to centered awareness.

*I*dentify what you're actually feeling beneath the surface. Are you angry? Or are you hurt? Disappointed? Scared? Lonely? Confused? The more specific you can get about your emotions, the clearer your communication will be.

*S*tories that might be running in your head need to be examined. Are you telling yourself, "He doesn't care about me" or "I always mess things up"? Notice these narratives without believing them completely. They're often more about old wounds than current reality.

*E*quilibrate by balancing your emotional narrative with facts. Yes, you feel disconnected from Alex right now. AND he's been working long hours on an important project. Both can be true. This isn't about dismissing your feelings; it's about creating space for complexity.

The whole **R.A.I.S.E.** process takes only 3-5 minutes. That's it. But those few minutes can mean the difference between an attack and an invitation, between disconnection and discovery.

Frequently Asked Coaching Question

"But Jenn, what if I don't have time to step away in the middle of a heated conversation?"

Totally fair question. Life doesn't always give you a convenient pause button. And let's be honest, you're probably not going to yell, "R.A.I.S.E. BREAK!" and run off to the bathroom mid-fight with your partner. *(Though honestly, it might break the tension if you did. Try it out and report back).*

The key is that removing yourself doesn't have to mean physically leaving the room. Sometimes it's as simple as saying, "I need a minute to think," or "Can we take a short break and come back to this?" And sometimes, removing just means going quiet for a few seconds instead of jumping in with a reaction. That pause is a form of removing.

Then you anchor. Not with full-on meditation, but with something small and accessible. Feel your feet on the floor. Notice the weight of your body in the seat of the car. Take a few deep breaths. Look around and name three things you see. That's it. It doesn't have to be fancy, it just has to bring you back to your body.

The goal isn't to feel perfectly calm. It's to get present enough to remember you have choices. Even if you do nothing else in the R.A.I.S.E. method, simply slowing down your breath and grounding into your body can shift the entire trajectory of a conversation. You're not trying to win. You're trying to stay.

Step 2: Validate (The 6 and 9 Analogy)

Once you're regulated, the next step is validation but probably not the way you think.

Most people think validation means agreeing with someone or telling them they're right. But that's not it at all. Validation is about seeing and acknowledging someone's perspective, even when it's different from yours. Dr. Marshall Rosenberg, creator of Nonviolent Communication, emphasized that this kind of empathic listening is one of the most powerful tools for creating connection, even in conflict.[3]

I like to use the **6 and 9 analogy**. Imagine the number 6 written on the ground between two people. One person sees a 6, the other sees a 9. They're both looking at the same thing, but from different perspectives. Neither is wrong. They're just seeing from where they stand.

Validation is saying, "I can see how, from where you're standing, that looks like a 9 to you." *(Even if you DON'T see it.)* You're not agreeing that it IS a 9. You're acknowledging their perspective as valid from their position.

What validation sounds like:

- "I can see why that would feel overwhelming to you."
- "That makes sense given what you're dealing with at work."
- "I understand why my tone came across as critical."
- "Of course you'd feel frustrated about that, I would too."

What validation is NOT:

- Fixing or solving their problem
- Agreeing with everything they say
- Taking responsibility for their emotions
- Dismissing your own perspective

When Alex got defensive about Maya's accusations, he saw a 9. To him, it felt like he was under attack and totally misunderstood. Meanwhile, Maya saw a 6. She wasn't trying to launch missiles; she was just worried and feeling a little disconnected. Both of their perspectives made sense from where they were standing. That's the wild thing about conflict, two people can be in the same room, have the same conversation, and still feel like they're living on different planets.

Imagine if Maya had started with a little validation, something like, "I can see how my tone came across as attacking and how that wouldn't feel good," the whole thing could have flipped. Instead of gearing up for battle, Alex might have exhaled. Instead of feeling more alone, Maya might have felt closer. It's not magic, but it really can be that simple. One small shift in words can move you from rupture to repair.

Frequently Asked Coaching Question

"But Jenn, what if I really don't agree with them?
How can I validate without lying?"

Let's be clear: **validation is not agreement.** It's not cosigning bad behavior or pretending you don't have your own view. Validation is saying, "I see where you're coming from, even if I don't live there."

You're not handing over the moral high ground. You're just acknowledging that, based on their thoughts, emotions, and lived experience, it makes sense why they feel what they feel. That's not lying. That's empathy.

Think about it like this: if they're seeing a 9 and you're seeing a 6, it doesn't help to scream, "YOU'RE WRONG!" It helps to say, "Ah, from where you're standing, I get why it looks that way." That creates **connection**. And connection is what makes your perspective more receivable too.

Step 3: Collaborate (From Criticism to Invitation)

The final step is shifting from blame or criticism to collaborative problem-solving. This is where you move from "you always" and "you never" statements to "we" language and solution-focused requests.

Instead of: "You never text me when you're going to be late!"
Try: "I'd love to find a way for us to stay connected when work gets busy. What would work for you?"

Instead of: "Why is it so hard for you to just listen to me?!"
Try: "I have something important to share. When would be a good time to talk?"

Instead of: "You always leave your dishes in the sink!"
Try: "I'd feel so supported if we could figure out a system for kitchen cleanup that works for both of us."

Notice how this collaborative approach completely shifts the energy of the conversation. Instead of focusing on who is "right" or "wrong," it places the spotlight on the relationship itself. It's not me versus you. It's us. It's we. That shift may seem small, but it instantly changes the tone from blame to connection.

Another key part of collaboration is the way requests are framed. Rather than coming in with demands that feel heavy-handed, the collaborative approach softens the edges by turning them into requests. Requests keep the door open for dialogue and say, "I value your input, and I want us to work this out together."

When you invite partnership in this way, you create space for the other person to contribute solutions of their own. People are far more invested in outcomes they had a hand in shaping, and a collaborative style doesn't just solve the immediate issue, it strengthens the trust that will matter the next time conflict arises.

The most important part to remember is that this isn't about being overly "nice" or pretending conflict doesn't exist. True collaboration doesn't sweep tension under the rug. When you approach someone as a **teammate** rather than an adversary, they're much more likely to lean in with openness instead of putting their defenses up. That's how repair and growth happen in relationships.

Frequently Asked Coaching Question

"Isn't it just giving in if I shift to 'we' language
when I'm the one who's hurt?"

Oof, I felt that one. It can definitely **feel** like you're doing the emotional heavy lifting, especially if you're the one initiating the hard conversations. But let me tell you using "we" language isn't weakness. It's leadership.

You're not giving up your needs, but rather, you're raising the bar for the relationship. When you say, "I want us to feel more connected," you're not minimizing your pain, you're inviting them into repair. That takes *strength*.

Criticism keeps you stuck in the past. Collaboration helps you build the future. And when done right, "we" language isn't soft. It's powerful. It's you saying, "I refuse to burn this thing down. I want to build something better."

Putting the Steps Together: Maya's Confidence

Three weeks after the "fight to end all fights" conversation, Maya called me with a very different story.

"I actually used the Regulate, Validate, Collaborate system last night," she said, and I could hear the pride in her voice. "Alex came home late again, and I felt that familiar anxiety spike. But instead of going into attack mode, I used that raise method you taught me."

"Tell me what that looked like," I said.

"First, I removed myself to the bathroom for literally two minutes. I felt my feet on the tile floor and took some deep breaths to anchor myself. Then I identified what I was actually feeling, which was sad and angry. I noticed the story I was telling myself about him was that he doesn't care about me, and I equilibrated that by reminding myself that he just filled up my gas tank the other day and he's been stressed about this work deadline."

"That's amazing! What happened next?"

"When I came out, instead of attacking him, I validated his experience first. I said, 'You look exhausted my love. Rough day at work?' He immediately softened and told me about everything that had gone wrong. Then we were able to work together."

"What did collaboration look like?"

"I told him I'd been looking forward to seeing him all day and was feeling a bit sad about being disconnected. It wasn't even about him being late, that really doesn't bother me. I just... miss him. I asked if we could have fifteen minutes to just check in with each other when he gets home. He said yes immediately, apologized for his work stuff and suggested we sit together and cuddle for a few minutes before doing anything else for now on."

Maya paused. "Jenn, it was like talking to a completely different man. Or maybe I was a completely different person? We ended up having the closest conversation we'd had in weeks."

That's the power of this system. Maya didn't become a different person; she just learned to communicate from her wisdom instead of her wounds.

MY OWN COMMUNICATION JOURNEY

My story began with one of the lowest moments of my life. In the middle of a painful conversation with someone I loved, I completely lost control. I yelled, and in a split second I can never take back, I **slapped** her. I'm not proud of that moment, but it's the truth of where I started. I was fiery and reactive, unsure how to express myself without chaos.

Years later, when that same conversation resurfaced *(because these things don't just disappear, annoyingly enough),* I had been doing the work to heal my wounds, understand my needs, and learn how to communicate with confidence. If I hadn't, I know it would have ended just as badly, if not worse.

Instead, something different happened. I was genuinely curious about her perspective. I wanted to understand what was going on for her. The shift was remarkable. Instead of being triggered and reactive, I was actually interested in learning more about how she saw the situation.

It wasn't like I didn't get triggered though. There was one moment she said something, and I felt my body get heated. Blood rushed to my face, my hands started shaking, that familiar surge of rage was building. But instead of exploding, I used **R.A.I.S.E.** in real time.

"I need to use the bathroom real quick," I said, **Removing** myself from the conversation.

I **Anchored** myself by feeling my feet on the cold tile floor, and took some big, deep breaths. I **Identified** what I was feeling, which was really hurt and confused. The **Story** I was telling myself was that she wasn't hearing me and that she didn't care about me.

When I started to **Equilibrate**, all the previous work I had done to alleviate my Attachment Wounds kicked in. My nervous system remembered: *I am heard,* and *I do matter.* I have people who listen to me and value me. This one conversation, even if she couldn't hear me, wouldn't change that truth.

When I went back out there, I validated her experience. Which was honestly one of the hardest things I've ever had to do because I don't think I'll ever truly see her side. But I can respect that she sees it that way, and I can acknowledge that her perspective makes sense from where she's standing. *(She sees the 6, I see the 9.)*

The ability to **Regulate** with the R.A.I.S.E. method helped me stay level-headed enough to **Validate** her. And once I validated her, the tension dropped just enough for us to begin **Collaborating**. From there, we could look at what we both needed and find a way forward that allowed us both to move on with our lives.

And let me tell you, that's no small thing. Old me would have stormed off, been crying in the bathroom, rage-texting a group chat, and stress-eating a whole sheet cake. New me? I stayed, kept my cool, and had a Secure conversation. Healing doesn't mean you never get triggered it means you stop letting the trigger run the whole damn show. That's the glow-up, girl. That's the work paying off.

Will our relationship look like it did before? Not at all, and I will need to grieve that. But grief doesn't mean defeat. It means I'm honoring what was; while choosing what's next. It means I can let go without losing myself.

YOUR CONFIDENT COMMUNICATION HOMEWORK

Ready to transform how you communicate? This isn't about memorizing scripts or becoming someone you're not. It's about developing skills that allow your authentic self to show up clearly, even in difficult moments.

Practice the R.A.I.S.E. Method Daily

For the next two weeks, practice R.A.I.S.E. in low-stakes situations. Don't wait for a major conflict to try this, build the muscle memory when things are calm.

Set a reminder on your phone to pause three times a day and run through **R.A.I.S.E.**

- **Remove**: Step away from what you're doing for 30 seconds.
- **Anchor**: Feel your feet, take three breaths, look around.
- **Identify**: Name what you're feeling in this moment.
- **Stories**: Notice any narratives running in your head.
- **Equilibrate**: Balance those stories with facts.

This might feel silly at first. You might think, *I'm not even upset about anything right now.* Do it anyway. Practicing when you're calm makes it easier to use later, kind of like rehearsing lines before the big show. The more you do it in those low-stakes moments, the more natural it becomes when emotions are running high. You're training your nervous system to access this tool automatically when you actually need it.

The more you practice in small moments, the more available this tool becomes during big moments.

Learn to Validate Perspectives

This week, practice validation with everyone, your partner, friends, family, even strangers. Look for opportunities to acknowledge someone else's perspective without fixing, agreeing, or defending.

Validation practice phrases:

- "That sounds really frustrating."
- "I can see why you'd feel that way."
- "That makes sense given what you're dealing with."
- "Of course you'd be upset about that."
- "I understand why that would be important to you."

Notice your urge to fix, explain, or offer solutions. Resist it. Just validate first. See what happens to the energy of the conversation when someone feels truly seen and understood.

Reframe One Criticism into Collaboration

Think about one ongoing issue in your relationship. Something you've complained about or criticized before. This week, practice reframing it as a collaborative request.

Examples:

- "You never help with housework." → "I'd love to figure out a way to share household tasks. What are your thoughts?"

- "You're always on your phone." → "I would love some time together. Wanna try a phone-free dinner?"

- "You don't understand me." → "I have something important to share. When would it be a good time to have a conversation where we can both feel heard?"

165

Notice how different it feels in your body to approach someone as a teammate rather than an opponent. Notice how they respond differently when you're inviting collaboration rather than issuing complaints.

Communication is a skill, not a talent. The more you practice these tools, the more natural they become. Soon, you'll find yourself automatically pausing to regulate, instinctively validating others' perspectives, and naturally approaching conflicts as opportunities for collaboration rather than threats to defend against.

Your relationships are about to get a whole lot more satisfying.

Remember, communication isn't just about knowing what to say in the moment; it's about all the work you do surrounding that moment that matters.

So be sure to keep up your daily Somatic Affirmation practice and keep nurturing your needs, because when you've been telling your nervous system "I am important" for weeks, it can regulate faster during conflict. When you know your needs and have been meeting them yourself, you can express them clearly instead of hoping someone will read your mind.

That's what made it possible for Maya to ask for connection instead of criticizing Alex. She wasn't just reacting. She'd done the deeper work that made real, conscious communication possible.

This isn't just homework. It's where your communication begins to move in step with your healing.

Need a Little Backup for the Hard Talks?

This workbook is your backup plan for the hard talks. Inside you'll find conversation scripts for when your brain freezes, exercises to sharpen your communication skills, a refresher on the R.A.I.S.E. Method, and a deeper dive into identifying your feelings. Real-life convos don't usually go by the book... but it helps to have one when things get messy.

Scan the QR code or get it at:
danceofattachment.com/workbook

Nine

EMBODY SECURE ATTACHMENT

*That's what it means to embody Secure Attachment.
You trust your ability to return to yourself.*

"I need to come in for a tune-up."

My phone pings, and there's a message from a client I haven't seen in over a year.

When Ava's face appears on my laptop screen the following Tuesday, I almost do a double-take. Gone is the girl with the frantic energy I remember from our sessions three years ago. The way she used to lean into the camera like she was trying to climb through the screen to get closer to the answers. Today, she's sitting back in what looks like a cozy reading nook, natural light streaming across her face, looking like someone who actually sleeps through the night.

"Okay, so," she begins, tucking one leg underneath her, "Will and I had our first real fight about wedding planning last weekend. And here's what's wild... I felt my whole system want to go into 'Oh my God, he's pulling away and this is all falling apart' mode, but I actually caught it happening."

She gestures with her hands as she talks, and there's something different about her movement—less frenetic, more grounded. "I literally felt my chest get tight and my breath get shallow, and instead of my usual spiral, I was like, 'Oh, hello abandonment wound, there you are.' Like I was greeting an old friend I haven't seen in a while."

I'm leaning forward now, captivated. The Ava I remember would have been sobbing by this point, convinced that one disagreement meant Will was shutting down and pulling away like he used to do in those early months of dating.

"So I told Will I needed twenty minutes to get myself together. Which, by the way, he was totally fine with because he's not the same guy who used to disappear for days when we had conflict, and I went for a walk around the block. The whole time I kept telling myself, 'Couples fight about wedding planning, Ava. This is normal. This doesn't mean he's checking out.'"

She pauses to take a sip from a white mug with the word *Bride* scripted in gold across the front. It's probably tea, but the way she holds it feels more like a grounding ritual than a beverage. "When I came back, he actually initiated the conversation to work through it. Three years ago, he would have just gone silent and hoped it would blow over."

I'm watching her tell this story and marveling at the woman in front of me. This is the same person who used to call me crying because Will had gone quiet for half a day after she brought up wanting to spend more time together.

"The thing is," Ava continues, "I can feel myself wanting to default to my old pattern of just agreeing with whatever he wants to avoid him withdrawing. And I know that's not fair to either of us anymore. So I was hoping we could practice how I can advocate for what I need... and see if any hidden wounds are kicking around in there."

She looks directly into the camera with clear, steady eyes. "I just want to make sure I'm asking for what I need from a place of love, not from my wound. And I want to honor how much work he's done too."

I sit back in my chair, blown away. This is what healing in action looks like. Not the absence of triggers, but a completely different relationship with them. Not perfection, but presence. Not avoiding your patterns, but dancing with them consciously.

"Tell me more about what you felt in your body when that familiar pattern wanted to take over," I say, ready to witness a woman who's learning to embody Secure Attachment. Not by avoiding conflict, but by accepting *(and dare I say welcoming?)* it.

WHAT DOES IT MEAN TO EMBODY BEING SECURE?

Embodying Secure Attachment means your healing isn't just something you **know**, it's something you **live**. It's in the way you breathe through a trigger instead of collapsing. It's in the way you pause before reacting, speak from your needs instead of your wounds, and stay present in the face of discomfort.

You're not just **thinking** differently. You're **being** differently.

Dr. Scott Lyons, somatic psychologist and founder of The Embody Lab, defines embodiment as "awareness of your internal experience and the ability to stay present with it." This includes your emotions, your body cues, your stories, and your sense of self. According to Dr. Lyons, true healing happens when we move from cognitive insight to **felt integration**.[1] In other words, we can stay with our experience without needing to run from it, fix it, or numb it.

That's the core of Secure Attachment, too. Secure people aren't unbothered... they're attuned. They can feel the swell of a trigger and still stay rooted. They can name a need without apology. They can even disagree without fearing abandonment.

Dr. Bessel van der Kolk, author of *The Body Keeps the Score*, says that trauma is not just stored in the mind—it's stored in the **body**.[2] When our Attachment Wounds are unhealed, our bodies react as if every conflict is a threat. Embodying Secure Attachment means we've taught our nervous system that we can survive closeness, that we can stay connected to ourselves even when connection with someone else feels wobbly.

And as Dr. Dan Siegel writes, Secure Attachment develops through consistent attunement.[3] When we embody security, we're attuned not just to others but to ourselves. We can say, "I'm feeling overwhelmed. I need a moment," instead of pretending we're fine or blowing up. We stop abandoning ourselves when things get hard.

This isn't about being perfect. You'll still have moments when your old patterns flare up. You'll still get flooded, or Avoidant, or Anxious sometimes. But instead of spiraling, you **notice**. You breathe. You come back.

That's what it means to embody Secure Attachment. You trust your ability to return to yourself.

HOW TO EMBODY SECURE ATTACHMENT

There is no step-by-step guide to embodying Secure Attachment. There's no checklist you can complete, no final exam you can pass, no graduation ceremony where someone hands you a certificate that says, "Congratulations, you've officially earned Secure Attachment!" *(Though if you want, I'll happily make you a cute certificate you can hang on your bathroom mirror. Just say the word.)*

Embodiment is what happens when you stop trying to **do** the work... and start **being** the work. Remember, you are not a human **doing**. You are a human **being**.

You've already learned the tools. You've discovered your Attachment Stance. You're actively working on alleviating your Attachment Wounds with your daily 15-minute Somatic Affirmation practice. You're nurturing your Attachment Needs by understanding them, meeting them, and receiving them. You can now communicate like the confident bad ass you are by Regulating before a big conversation, Validating during it, and Collaborating so everyone feels safe, seen, and secure in the relationship.

Now? You live your life. You make mistakes. You try new things. You keep going.

And here's what nobody tells you about the journey: Each time you level up in life, you're going to feel those familiar Attachment feelings again. Feeling Secure while you're single, but now Anxious in a new relationship? Great! You leveled up! Feeling Secure in your new relationship, but now you're nervous about moving in together? Awesome! You leveled up again! Comfortable living together, but panicking about engagement? Perfect! Another level up!

Each milestone, each new experience, each deeper level of intimacy is going to activate your Attachment system. That doesn't mean you're broken. That doesn't mean you're not healing. That doesn't mean you're doing this wrong. It means you've reached a place in your life where you're brave enough to try hard mode. And I'm proud of you for that.

The embodiment happens in how you meet these moments. Not with shame about feeling triggered, but with **compassion** for the part of you that's scared of this new territory. Not by avoiding the growth, but by **breathing** through it. Not by abandoning yourself when things get hard, but by **staying present** with your own experience.

That was what Ava was doing in our opening story. She felt the old panic trying to take over, and instead of spiraling or shutting down, she noticed it, named it, took care of herself, and then showed up for the conversation from a regulated place.

That's embodiment. Not the absence of activation, but the presence with it.

MY OWN EMBODIMENT STORY

The paper bib was already clipped around my neck when it started.

I was lying in the dentist's chair getting a cavity filled *(one I had noped out of for 14 years)* when suddenly my heart started racing. My chest got tight. My throat closed. That familiar feeling of being trapped, vulnerable, and out of control crashed over me like a wave.

This wasn't just about the dentist. It was every medical procedure that had gone wrong, every childhood moment when I couldn't escape, every time my body screamed *DANGER!* and no one listened.

My eyes welled up with tears, and I had this surge of panic. I'd had some anxiety during my recent cleanings, but this was different. This was terror. My body was reliving every moment where it had ever felt powerless.

What was happening that day wasn't logical. I knew I was safe. I knew I was okay. I knew I was in control. But as we've talked about so many times throughout this book, my body wasn't reacting to the present moment. It was reacting to all the times in the past I was forced to stay in a situation that hurt me. So, of course, it makes sense that I still felt fear. And that's okay.

Old me would've shoved those feelings down, forced myself to get through the appointment, smiled politely, and then cried in the car on the way home. *(And then ghosted the dentist like a bad Tinder date for the next 14 years.)* I would've told myself I was overreacting, that it was no big deal, that I was being too sensitive.

But that day? I did something **different**.

I raised my hand, sat up in the chair, and said, "I'm actually feeling really anxious right now. Can I take a minute?" The dental hygienist was kind. She handed me water, gave me space, and let me be human. I didn't feel embarrassed. I felt proud. I could have left. Hell, I almost did. But the decision to stay was mine. I was in control. I had the power.

When I needed another break, I asked to go to the bathroom. The dentist made a snide comment about how long it was taking. I could've spiraled into shame or panic. Instead, I said, "Thank you for your patience," and went to the bathroom and sobbed.

I might have been sobbing, but I stayed with myself. I didn't abandon my body to make someone else comfortable. I didn't judge my fear or try to fix it. I listened. I breathed. And, in that moment, something shifted.

That's **embodied** Secure Attachment.

It's not about staying calm all the time. It's not about never being triggered. It's about recognizing the signal, naming the need, and responding with compassion. It's staying with the parts of you that were once too scared to speak.

At that moment *(sitting upright in a paper bib, sipping water like it was a post-battle whiskey in a war movie flashback)*, I knew something was rewiring. Not because I was calm. Not because I looked healed. But because I chose to stay with myself through the fear. I didn't override my body's signals. I didn't shrink. I didn't run.

I stayed.

And in that choice, I gave myself something I had always needed as a child—proof that I was safe to be exactly who I am. That I could feel everything and still be worthy of care. That I didn't have to abandon myself just to get through something hard. That I had my own back now.

That's what embodied Secure Attachment looks like.

It's not about perfection. It's not about always being regulated. It's about staying with yourself, even when everything in you wants to disappear.

It's about facing fear with tenderness and choosing yourself each time you do.

Even in a paper bib.

YOUR EMBODIEMENT HOMEWORK

This is it. Your final homework assignment. Are you ready?

Dance.

That's it. That's the whole thing.

I want you to live your life like it's a dance floor.
Show up like the lead in your own choreography.
Twirl into the joy.
Sway through the hard days.
Two-step with your triggers.
Make choices like you're building the perfect Spotify playlist.

You already know the steps. Now it's time to stop counting and just feel the music.

This is your dance now. Own it. Live it.

Dance like no one's watching, because honestly, who gives a flying fuck if they are? Let them watch girl and let them admire you as you become everything you were always meant to be.

LAST DANCE

LAST CHANCE FOR LOVE

*"Will you be my Mr. Right? Can you fill my appetite?
I can't be sure that you're the one for me. But all that
I ask is that you dance with me."*
— Donna Summer

LAST CALL ON THE DANCE FLOOR

Look, I'm not gonna give you some shiny, inspirational farewell speech. You made it to the end of this book. That already tells me you're a badass. You've danced with your demons. You've sat with your shame. You've looked your childhood in the eye and said, "Okay, let's talk."

That's not easy. That's not light work. That's the heavy, sweaty, ugly-cry-on-the-bathroom-floor kind of work. And if no one has told you lately, I'm proud of you. Like, for real.

I don't care if you're still texting your ex, even though you know he's emotionally constipated and allergic to accountability. I don't care if you just spiraled because someone took three hours to text you back. I truly don't care if your Attachment Stance is still pulling some real dramatic bullshit every time you start to like someone.

We've all been there. I **have** been there. That's why I wrote this book.

But now you know better. And knowing better doesn't mean you'll never do something messy again. It means you'll catch it faster. You'll see it for what it is. You'll stop making it mean something about your worth. You'll pause and go, "Okay, that was some classic stupid shit right there... but I see it now."

And that's the shift.

That's how smart women stop doing dumb shit in relationships. Not by getting it right every time but by staying conscious while it's happening. Not by chasing perfection but by showing up present, self-aware, and real.

You don't ghost yourself anymore just to keep someone else around. You don't make yourself smaller just to be chosen. You don't abandon your body to keep the peace. You still fuck up sometimes. We all do. But now, you know why. And you know what to do next.

And let me just say this again for the people in the back... you do not NEED a partner. You get to **choose** one. You get to choose someone who doesn't just tolerate your truth but celebrates it.

So go out there. Try. Mess up. Learn. Love big. Cry when it's hard. Laugh when it's ridiculous. Say too much. Pull back when you need to. Take a beat. Take a breath. Take the lead. And when you forget the steps? Just remember... your body knows the rhythm now.

You're not broken. You're becoming.

Becoming is messy. It's clumsy, it's awkward, and half the time you'll wonder if you're even doing it right. But here's the thing, that's the point! Healing isn't about never tripping over your own two feet again. It's about getting back up, brushing yourself off, and keeping time with the music anyway. Every stumble is proof you're becoming.

And babes, you're becoming Secure as Fuck. (*Coming soon to a bookshelf near you. Just kidding. Unless...*)

ACKNOWLEDGMENTS

To the Reader

If you made it here, I hope you know how proud I am of you. You could've picked up any book, but you chose this one. You stayed. You turned the pages. You danced with me through the mess. Whether you cried, laughed, cursed, or threw the damn book across the room *(honestly, valid)*, I'm so fucking grateful you're here. I am honored to be a part of your healing journey and from the bottom of my heart, thank you for being a part of mine.

To My Reboot Girlies

You showed me what's possible when healing meets community. You didn't just inspire this book... you're woven into every word of it. Watching your growth reminded me to keep growing too. Thank you for trusting me, for trusting yourselves, and for reminding me why this work matters.

To the Man I Continue To Choose

You are my Secure base. Thank you for loving me gently, fiercely, and without conditions. For choosing fairness over fantasy. For showing up, not just when it was easy, but when it mattered most. I am forever grateful that you knew what was fair for *you* and still chose *us*.

To My Son

Being your mom is the greatest honor of my life. You are the reason I fight for a world where voices are heard and people are believed. You inspire me every single day, just by being exactly who you are and bravely becoming who you're meant to be. I am so proud of you.

To My Besties

You sat with me through the breakdowns, the breakthroughs, and the never-ending Google Docs. You reminded me who I was when I forgot. You listened to every rant, celebrated every win, and held me steady through every spiral. You are the kind of friends who make a woman believe she can do anything. Even write a whole damn book. Thank you for being my soft place to land, my hype squad, my chosen family. I love you more than words *(and that's saying something, because I used a lot of them here).*

To Lucky Book Publishing

You've created something rare. A community that doesn't just make books, but makes magic. Thank you to the fellow authors who lifted me up, the friends I've made, and the ones I haven't met yet.

To My Amazing Assistant

You're the reason I stay *(mostly)* sane. Thank you for showing up every week with calm, clarity, and a sense of humor that gets me through the madness. You're more than an assistant, you're a steady force, a thought partner, and a mama walking a parallel path beside me. I'm so grateful we're growing through this together. I can't wait to see where this wild ride takes us both.

To My Professors

You reminded me that I don't have to sound polished to have something worth saying. Thank you for seeing the writer in me when all I saw was a dropout with a lot of feelings.

To My Editor and Graphic Designer

You both took my wild ideas and turned them into a book I'm proud of. You helped me feel seen in my own voice, and that is a rare gift.

To the Pandemic

Yep, I'm actually putting you in here. You kicked my ass. You stripped everything away. And somehow, in the ruins, you handed me this new life. I never saw it coming, but I'm here now, and I wouldn't change it.

To All the Boys I Have Loved Before

Thank you for loving me when you did. Thank you for breaking me open. I couldn't have written this book without you.

To the Ones Who Shaped Me

It all started with Thais Gibson, on a hot night in May. I was curled up in bed, half-distracted with a snack and a White Claw, when I stumbled across her explanation of Attachment Styles. For the first time, something inside of me finally clicked. Thais has a gift for pulling together information from different sources and laying it out in a way that makes it easy to understand. And I will be forever grateful for that. Thais, you changed my life *(yes, I know you'd say I changed it)*, but your work lit the match.

To the brilliant forces of nature who cracked me open and rebuilt my understanding of trauma and healing: Dr. Gabor Maté, Dr. Richard Schwartz, Dr. Scott Lyons, Dr. Peter Levine, Dr. Diane Poole Heller and Dr. Bessel van der Kolk. Thank you for being the giants I've had the honor to learn from. Training under each of you has been one long pinch-me moment, and I still can't quite believe I get to carry your work forward in my own way. One day, I hope to add my own research to the field you've built.

Thank you for teaching me. For challenging me. And for making it impossible to go back to who I was before.

To Mary Ainsworth and Mary Main

You are the two badass women who took Attachment Theory to the next level. I hope to follow in your footsteps someday... even if my name isn't Mary *(but honestly, if that's what it takes, I'll consider it).*

To Mission College

You let a disoriented, drunk, high, heartbroken woman sign up for classes on a random Tuesday night... and you changed her life. You gave me a home. You gave me a family. You gave me my TEDx talk. You gave me a new story. You gave me my Mission.

And Finally

To the White Claws and Chocolate Bars. You were my besties when I needed to survive. I may not need you as much anymore, but you'll always be there for me, whispering that I deserve better than you, and for that, you will always hold a special place in my heart.

ENDNOTES

(Those little numbers)

PART ONE

Before We Dance

1. John Bowlby, *A Secure Base: Parent-Child Attachment and Healthy Human Development* (New York: Basic Books, 1988).

2. Mary D. S. Ainsworth, Mary C. Blehar, Everett Waters, and Sally Wall, *Patterns of Attachment: A Psychological Study of the Strange Situation* (Hillsdale, NJ: Erlbaum, 1978).

3. Mary Main and Judith Solomon, "Procedures for Identifying Infants as Disorganized/Disoriented During the Ainsworth Strange Situation," in *Attachment in the Preschool Years: Theory, Research, and Intervention*, ed. Mark T. Greenberg, Dante Cicchetti, and E. Mark Cummings (Chicago: University of Chicago Press, 1990), 121—160.

4. Daniel J. Siegel, *The Developing Mind: How Relationships and the Brain Interact to Shape Who We Are*, 2nd ed. (New York: Guilford Press, 2012).

5. Louis Cozolino, *The Neuroscience of Psychotherapy: Healing the Social Brain*, 3rd ed. (New York: W. W. Norton & Company, 2017).

One: Salsa Of Uncertainty | Anxious Attachment

1. Mary D. S. Ainsworth, Mary C. Blehar, Everett Waters, and Sally Wall, *Patterns of Attachment: A Psychological Study of the Strange Situation* (Hillsdale, NJ: Erlbaum, 1978), 129.

2. Cindy Hazan and Phillip R. Shaver, "Romantic Love Conceptualized as an Attachment Process," *Journal of Personality and Social Psychology* 52, no. 3 (1987): 511—524.

3. Louis Cozolino, *The Neuroscience of Psychotherapy: Healing the Social Brain*, 3rd ed. (New York: W. W. Norton & Company, 2017).

4. Gabor Maté, *When the Body Says No: Exploring the Stress-Disease Connection* (Hoboken, NJ: Wiley, 2003).

5. Jean-Philippe Gouin, Ronald Glaser, William B. Malarkey, David Beversdorf, and Janice Kiecolt-Glaser, "Attachment Avoidance Predicts Inflammatory Responses to Marital Conflict," *Brain, Behavior, and Immunity* 24, no. 1 (2010): 16—21.

6. Phillip R. Shaver and Mario Mikulincer, "Attachment-Related Psychodynamics," *Attachment & Human Development* 4, no. 2 (2002): 133—161.

7. John Bowlby, *A Secure Base: Parent-Child Attachment and Healthy Human Development* (New York: Basic Books, 1988).

8. Brené Brown, *The Gifts of Imperfection* (Center City, MN: Hazelden, 2010).

9. Sue Johnson, *Hold Me Tight: Seven Conversations for a Lifetime of Love* (New York: Little, Brown Spark, 2008).

10. Phillip R. Shaver, Nancy Collins, and Carol L. Clark, "Being Lonely, Falling in Love: Perspectives from Attachment Theory," in *The Art of Integrative Counseling*, ed. C. S. Watkins and D. L. Barone (Pacific Grove, CA: Brooks/Cole Publishing, 1996), 29—45.

11. Donald O. Hebb, *The Organization of Behavior: A Neuropsychological Theory* (New York: Wiley, 1949).

Two: Solo Tango | Avoidant Attachment

1. Cindy Hazan and Phillip R. Shaver, "Romantic Love Conceptualized as an Attachment Process," *Journal of Personality and Social Psychology* 52, no. 3 (1987): 511—524.

2. Mary D. S. Ainsworth, Mary C. Blehar, Everett Waters, and Sally Wall, *Patterns of Attachment: A Psychological Study of the Strange Situation* (Hillsdale, NJ: Erlbaum, 1978).

3. Naomi I. Eisenberger, Matthew D. Lieberman, and Kipling D. Williams, "Do Neural Responses to Rejection Depend on Attachment Style? An fMRI Study," *Psychological Science* 14, no. 5 (2003): 409—414.

4. Stephen W. Porges, *The Polyvagal Theory: Neurophysiological Foundations of Emotions, Attachment, Communication, and Self-Regulation* (New York: W. W. Norton & Company, 2007).

5. Tara Kidd, Mark Hamer, and Andrew Steptoe, "Examining the

Association Between Adult Attachment Style and Cortisol Responses to Acute Stress," *Psychoneuroendocrinology* 36, no. 10 (2011): 1485—1493.

6. Kasia Kozlowska, Suzanne Scher, and Leanne M. Williams, "Patterns of Emotional-Cognitive Functioning in Pediatric Conversion Patients: Implications for the Conceptualization of Conversion Disorders," *Psychosomatic Medicine* 73, no. 4 (2011): 312—319.

7. Kyoung-Hee Koh and Sang-Hee Choi, "Sources of Somatization: Exploring the Roles of Insecurity in Attachment and Anger," *Journal of Clinical Psychology* 61, no. 10 (2005): 1329—1339.

8. Robin S. Edelstein and Omri Gillath, "Avoiding Interference: Adult Attachment and Emotional Processing," *Personality and Social Psychology Bulletin* 34, no. 2 (2008): 171—181.

9. Mario Mikulincer and Phillip R. Shaver, *Attachment in Adulthood: Structure, Dynamics, and Change* (New York: The Guilford Press, 2005).

10. Louis Cozolino, *The Neuroscience of Human Relationships: Attachment and the Developing Social Brain* (New York: W. W. Norton & Company, 2006).

Three: Pendulum Swing Dance | Disorganized Attachment

1. Mary Main and Judith Solomon, "Procedures for Identifying Infants as Disorganized/Disoriented During the Ainsworth Strange Situation," in *Attachment in the Preschool Years: Theory,*

Research, and Intervention, ed. Mark T. Greenberg, Dante Cicchetti, and E. Mark Cummings (Chicago: University of Chicago Press, 1990), 121—160.

2. Mary Main and Erik Hesse, "Parents' Unresolved Traumatic Experiences Are Related to Infant Disorganized Attachment Status: Is Frightened and/or Frightening Parental Behavior the Linking Mechanism?" in *Attachment in the Preschool Years: Theory, Research, and Intervention*, ed. Mark T. Greenberg, Dante Cicchetti, and E. Mark Cummings (Chicago: University of Chicago Press, 1990), 161—182.

3. Antje Buchheim et al., "Neural Correlates of Attachment Trauma in Borderline Personality Disorder: A Functional Magnetic Resonance Imaging Study," *Psychiatry Research: Neuroimaging* 163, no. 3 (2008): 223—235.

4. Bessel A. van der Kolk, *The Body Keeps the Score: Brain, Mind, and Body in the Healing of Trauma* (New York: Viking, 2014).

5. Stephen W. Porges, *The Polyvagal Theory: Neurophysiological Foundations of Emotions, Attachment, Communication, and Self-Regulation* (New York: W. W. Norton & Company, 2011).

6. George M. Slavich and Michael R. Irwin, "From Stress to Inflammation and Major Depressive Disorder: A Social Signal Transduction Theory of Depression," *Psychological Bulletin* 140, no. 3 (2014): 774—815.

7. Judith L. Herman, *Trauma and Recovery* (New York: Basic Books, 1992).

8. Amir Levine and Rachel Heller, *Attached: The New Science of Adult Attachment and How It Can Help You Find—and Keep—Love* (New York: TarcherPerigee, 2010).

9. Daniel J. Siegel, *The Developing Mind: How Relationships and the Brain Interact to Shape Who We Are*, 2nd ed. (New York: Guilford Press, 2012).

Four: Smooth Waltz | Secure Attachment

1. Sheri Madigan et al., "The First 20,000 Strange Situation Procedures: A Meta-Analytic Review," *Psychological Bulletin* 149, no. 1—2 (2023): 99—132, https://doi.org/10.1037/bul0000388.

2. Yayoi Minagawa-Kawai et al., "Prefrontal Activation Associated with Social Attachment: Facial-Emotion Recognition in Mothers and Infants," *Cerebral Cortex* 19, no. 2 (2008): 284—292, https://doi.org/10.1093/cercor/bhn081.

3. Stephen W. Porges, *The Polyvagal Theory: Neurophysiological Foundations of Emotions, Attachment, Communication, and Self-Regulation* (New York: W. W. Norton & Company, 2011).

4. Bessel A. van der Kolk, *The Body Keeps the Score: Brain, Mind, and Body in the Healing of Trauma* (New York: Viking, 2014).

5. Angelo Picardi et al., "Attachment Style and Immunity: A 1-Year Longitudinal Study," *Biological Psychology* 92, no. 2 (2013): 353—358, https://doi.org/10.1016/j.biopsycho.2012.10.001.

6. Lisa M. Jaremka et al., "Attachment Anxiety Is Linked to Altera-
    tions in Cortisol Production and Cellular Immunity,"
    Psychological Science 24, no. 3 (2013): 272—279,
    https://doi.org/10.1177/0956797612452571.

7. Tara Kidd, Mark Hamer, and Andrew Steptoe, "Examining the
    Association Between Adult Attachment Style and Cortisol Re-
    sponses to Acute Stress," *Psychoneuroendocrinology* 36, no. 6
    (2011): 771—779,
    https://doi.org/10.1016/j.psyneuen.2010.10.014.

8. Elizabeth Sloan et al., "Insecure Attachment Is Associated with
    the α-EEG Anomaly During Sleep," *BioPsychoSocial Medicine* 1,
    no. 1 (2007): 20, https://doi.org/10.1186/1751-0759-1-20.

9. Sue M. Johnson, *Attachment Theory in Practice: Emotionally Fo-
    cused Therapy (EFT) with Individuals, Couples, and Families*
    (New York: Guilford Press, 2019).

10. Mary Main, Nancy Kaplan, and Jude Cassidy, "Security in In-
    fancy, Childhood, and Adulthood: A Move to the Level of
    Representation," *Monographs of the Society for Research in
    Child Development* 50, no. 1—2 (1985): 66—104,
    https://doi.org/10.2307/3333827.

11. Edward Tronick et al., "The Infant's Response to Entrapment
    Between Contradictory Messages in Face-to-Face Interaction,"
    Journal of the American Academy of Child Psychiatry 17, no. 1
    (1978): 1—13, https://doi.org/10.1016/S0002-7138(09)62273-
    1.

12. Edward Tronick and Marjorie Beeghly, "Infants' Meaning-Making and the Development of Mental Health Problems," *American Psychologist* 66, no. 2 (2011): 107—119, https://doi.org/10.1037/a0021631.

13. D. W. Winnicott, "Transitional Objects and Transitional Phenomena: A Study of the First Not-Me Possession," *International Journal of Psycho-Analysis* 34 (1953): 89—97.

14. Mary Main and Ruth Goldwyn, "Predicting Rejection of Her Infant from Mother's Representation of Her Own Experience: Implications for the Abused-Abusing Intergenerational Cycle," *Child Abuse & Neglect* 8, no. 2 (1984): 203—217, https://doi.org/10.1016/0145-2134(84)90009-7.

15. Glenn I. Roisman et al., "Earned-Secure Attachment Status in Retrospect and Prospect," *Child Development* 73, no. 4 (2002): 1204—1219, https://doi.org/10.1111/1467-8624.00467.

16. Kristin D. Neff, "Self-Compassion: An Alternative Conceptualization of a Healthy Attitude Toward Oneself," *Self and Identity* 2, no. 2 (2003): 85—101, https://doi.org/10.1080/15298860309032.

PART TWO

Five: Discover Your Attachment Stance

1. Daniel J. Siegel, *The Developing Mind: How Relationships and the Brain Interact to Shape Who We Are*, 2nd ed. (New York: Guilford Press, 2012).

Six: Alleviate Your Attachment Wounds

1. Daniel J. Siegel, *The Developing Mind: How Relationships and the Brain Interact to Shape Who We Are*, 2nd ed. (New York: Guilford Press, 2012).

2. John Bowlby, *A Secure Base: Parent-Child Attachment and Healthy Human Development* (New York: Basic Books, 1988).

3. Allan N. Schore, *Affect Regulation and the Repair of the Self* (New York: W. W. Norton & Company, 2003).

4. Peter A. Levine, *Waking the Tiger: Healing Trauma* (Berkeley, CA: North Atlantic Books, 1997).

5. Mark P. Jensen, Tomonori Adachi, and Shaheen Hakimian, "Brain Oscillations, Hypnosis, and Hypnotizability," *American Journal of Clinical Hypnosis* 57, no. 3 (2015): 230—253, https://doi.org/10.1080/00029157.2014.976785.

6. Norman Doidge, *The Brain That Changes Itself: Stories of Personal Triumph from the Frontiers of Brain Science* (New York: Penguin Books, 2007).

7. Phillippa Lally et al., "How Are Habits Formed: Modelling Habit Formation in the Real World," *European Journal of Social Psychology* 40, no. 6 (2010): 998—1009.

Seven: Nurture Your Attachment Needs

1. John M. Gottman and Julie Schwartz Gottman, "The Natural Principles of Love," *Journal of Family Theory & Review* 9, no. 1 (2017): 7—26.

2. Tony Robbins, *Awaken the Giant Within: How to Take Immediate Control of Your Mental, Emotional, Physical and Financial Destiny!* (New York: Free Press, 1991).

Eight: Communicate With Confidence

1. John M. Gottman and Robert W. Levenson, "Marital Processes Predictive of Later Dissolution: Behavior, Physiology, and Health," *Journal of Personality and Social Psychology* 63, no. 2 (1992): 221—233.

2. Amy F. T. Arnsten, "Stress Signaling Pathways That Impair Prefrontal Cortex Structure and Function," *Nature Reviews Neuroscience* 10, no. 6 (2009): 410—422.

3. Marshall B. Rosenberg, *Nonviolent Communication: A Language of Life* (Encinitas, CA: PuddleDancer Press, 2003).

Nine: Embody Secure Attachment

1. Scott Lyons, *The Embody Lab Curriculum* (2022), accessed June 15, 2025, https://www.theembodylab.com.

2. Bessel A. van der Kolk, *The Body Keeps the Score: Brain, Mind, and Body in the Healing of Trauma* (New York: Viking, 2014).

3. Daniel J. Siegel, *The Developing Mind: How Relationships and the Brain Interact to Shape Who We Are*, 2nd ed. (New York: Guilford Press, 2012).

STAY CONNECTED

Your healing journey doesn't have to end here. What you've started in these pages is just the beginning. Healing isn't a one-and-done moment, it's a dance you get to keep practicing and deepening. The more you surround yourself with tools, stories, and community, the easier it becomes to stay connected to the secure, grounded version of yourself you've been working toward. That's why I've created spaces beyond this book where you can keep learning, growing, and connecting with me.

All-in-one Resource Hub
Go to *danceofattachment.com/resources* to find everything *(and more!)* mentioned in this book.

Watch the TEDx Talk
If you're a visual learner *(or just want to see me in full-on red dot realness)*, don't miss my TEDx talk: *Do Attachment Styles Determine the Dance of Our Relationships?* You can check out the official video at *danceofattachment.com/tedx*.

Listen to the Podcast
Looking for real talk on healing, relationships, and how to stop losing yourself in love? My podcast, *Speak Honest*, is your go-to podcast for real conversations about Attachment, boundaries, communication, nervous system stuff, and how to show up as your whole damn self. I bring the science, the stories, and sometimes a little sass. Listen at *speak-honest.com/podcast* or wherever you like to listen to podcasts.

Come Dance With Me

- **Instagram:** @speak_honest—where I post daily insights, voice-note realness, and occasional dance moves
- **Facebook**: *facebook.com/speakhonestcoach*—for updates, community convos, and live sessions
- **LinkedIn**: *linkedin.com/in/jennifer-noble-acc*—if you want to see the polished version of me
- **Website**: *speak-honest.com*—everything you need in one place
- **Email:** jennifer@speak-honest.com—questions, reflections, speaking invites, or just a note to say this book meant something to you? I'd truly love to hear it

Join the Community

Come hang out in ♥ *Speak Honest* ♥ *Secure Attachment and Confident Communication for Women.* Our free Facebook group for connection, support, and honest conversations. *facebook.com/groups/speakhonest*

Speaking Requests

For podcast interviews, stage events, or TV appearances, please visit *danceofattachment.com/speakingevents* or directly at jennifer@speak-honest.com

However we stay connected, just know this: you're not doing this alone anymore. I gotchu.

ABOUT THE AUTHOR

Jenn Noble is a TEDx speaker, Professional Certified Coach with the International Coaching Federation (ICF), founder of *Speak Honest* and host of the *Speak Honest Podcast*, where she helps women heal their Attachment Stance and stop doing dumb sh*t in the name of love. With advanced training in Integrated Attachment Theory (IAT), Neuro-Linguistic Programming (NLP), Compassionate Inquiry (CI), and Somatic Attachment Therapy (SAT)—plus degrees in Psychology, Communication Studies, and Social Justice—Jenn blends science and sass to help women become Secure in their relationships without losing themselves.

She is a big believer that healing doesn't happen when we play small. It happens when we speak up, love bravely, and learn to lead the dance. Jenn lives in California with her husband, son, cat, and bunny, who keep life just the right mix of grounded and chaotic.

BEFORE YOU GO...

Thank you for spending your time, your energy, and your heart on this book. I don't take that lightly.

If something in these pages moved you, helped you, or made you laugh-snort in public... **would you consider leaving a review on Amazon or Goodreads?**

It doesn't have to be long or fancy. Just honest. Just you.

Reviews help indie authors like me get these words into the hands of more women who need them. And if this book meant something to you? That means everything to me.

With love and gratitude,

Jenn

★ ★ ★ ★ ★

This book will absolutely change the way you see yourself and how you show up in relationships.

- Jordan H.

MY GIFT TO YOU

You've done the reading, now it's time to do the work.

The Dance of Attachment Companion Workbook is designed to guide you through Part Two of this journey and help you practice the D.A.N.C.E. steps for yourself.

Inside, you'll find the exercises, prompts, and tools that bring these pages off the paper and into your real life.

Ready to get started? Scan the QR code to download your copy or visit *danceofattachment.com/workbook.*

This book gives you the framework. The workbook helps you live it, one step at a time.

Scan Me

www.ingramcontent.com/pod-product-compliance
Lightning Source LLC
Chambersburg PA
CBHW021140130626
46554CB00005B/1589